THE MUSICAL WORLD OF PAUL WINTER

the musical world of

# Paul Winter

Bob Gluck

Terra Nova Editions

2025

# Table of Contents

This book is dedicated to Pamela Lerman
and in memory of David Darling and Susan Osborn.

# Foreword

As publisher of *Terra Nova Press*, I have had the honor of releasing many beautiful books on jazz, world, and improvised
music, from Elliott Sharp's *Irrational Music*, Benedicte
Maurseth's *To Be Nothing* to W.A. Matthieu's *The Shrine
Thief*. It pleases me to no end to be able to offer this revised,
first-ever print edition of Bob Gluck's meticulous study of
the great saxophonist and environmentalist Paul Winter,
who has had such an influence on me ever since I first heard
about his work making music with wolves, whales, and birds
as a teenager growing up in Connecticut. Winter lived a bit
upstate from me, and he was truly my hero, showing a clear
example of how one could combine a career in jazz with raising consciousness toward saving the Earth. In a way I have
modeled my own musical life upon his example.

There is no other book on Winter's extraordinary life
and work. I am happy to say he is still out there, playing his
pure-toned soprano saxophone with the many songs of the
Earth, bringing tears and smiles to audiences all over the
planet.

Let this fine work be an inspiration to many, as Winter's life has been to me.

*David Rothenberg, publisher*
*Terra Nova Press*

## Preface

Saxophonist/environmentalist Paul Winter first heard whale songs in 1968 on a recording played at a lecture by scientist Roger Payne. The talk took place at Rockefeller University, where Payne was assistant professor of physiology and animal behavior.

Winter listened closely as Payne played humpback whale recordings during his talk. He was deeply moved. "The whales' voices seemed to express to me something of the soul of the earth." He was stirred by their intelligence and musicality and concerned for their plight:

> In addition to the beauty of their voices, I was stunned by the level of intelligence these songs seemed to reflect and by the reality that these magnificent creatures were in danger of being exterminated by us. I heard that these creatures were being slaughtered for things like lipstick and dog food and I was ready to go to the front. A new facet of my life's mission came clear that day.

During the 1970s, Winter began to participate in whale watches and celebrations and organizational benefits for whale protection. But he thought that an experience trying to make music "with" whales would prove frustrating. He concluded that "somehow I wanted to share those sounds with people. Somehow I wanted to incorporate their sounds." In the mid-1970s, he learned about wolves and played music "communing" with whales.

Paul Winter doesn't consider himself an environmentalist although many people might argue with him on that point. He addresses issues about endangered species and environments from a place of love and empathy and his music is aesthetically beautiful and enchanting. He has a gift for melody and he speaks with infectious optimism. Listening to his lilting melodies based on the songs of the humpback whale or the howls of the timber wolf brings tears to the ears of his listeners. It is something one can experience by attending one of his concerts. Winter is able to guide audience members to let go of their inhibitions and howl en masse like a pack of wolves.

He traveled a fascinating path, from a small central Pennsylvania railroad town to an unexpected career as a college jazz musician in Chicago to touring South America at the invitation of the U.S. State Department and playing at the Kennedy White House. He played in Russia, recorded in the Grand Canyon, discovered the music of Brazil, organized a town party for Charles Ives' birthday. For his group, he adopted an Elizabethan English musical model known as the "Consort," a group of collaborative, talented, and expressive musicians who experimented with diverse musical forms. And he found new expression in his magnificent epic events at the Cathedral of St. John the Divine in New York City, beginning with an Earth Mass then, in successive years, becoming an annual Solstice Celebration with multi-media dramas of music, dance, lights, and storytelling.

It has been my fortune to have attended many performances by the Paul Winter Consort over the past four decades, as well as workshops by his partners David Darling and Susan Osborn. In fact, David, Susan, and Jim Scott have been indispensable in the writing of this book.

I have drawn upon the many published interviews given by Paul Winter during the 1970s-2000s, interviews I conducted with David Darling, Susan Osborn, and Jim Scott, published interviews by Ralph Towner, Glen Moore, Paul McCandless, and Collin Walcott, scholarly articles by whale and wolf researchers, and my own descriptions and reflections about Winter's recordings. I have appreciated Paul Winter's personal warmth as well as his creative energies, all of which have enriched my life.

I offer a lifetime of gratitude to composer and music historian, Joel Chadabe, in the late 1970s, my college teacher, and for two recent decades, a professional mentor and collaborator. Joel passed away in 2021, two years after publishing a first, ebook edition of this volume. I offer many thanks to David Rothenberg for his encouragement and, ultimately, production of this new edition on his Terra Nova imprint.

—*Bob Gluck*

Paul Winter has a wide-open receiver to most kinds of music. He has devoted many years to creating world music. It wasn't uncommon for us to gather at the St. John Cathedral in New York on a Tuesday before a concert and be introduced to an Armenian singer and an Irish *uileann* pipe player. They'd be introduced to each other and to us; this would be on a Tuesday and we'd all have to put together a concert to be performed on Thursday in front of thousands of people. It was just great. Paul would put all these wildly disparate elements together and gradually shape them into a whole; it would be "why don't you try this..." and "why not try that..." You might end up in fact with an *uileann* pipe and pipe organ improvisation. You don't hear that every day. We were all open to it. It's a great attribute of Paul's that he really flings his arms wide to different kinds of music in the world, and has faith that his musicians can make it happen.

—*Paul Sullivan,*
*pianist, Paul Winter Consort*

*Paul Winter at the Clearwater Festival, 2007, Croton-on-Hudson, NY*
*photo by Anthony Pepitone*

## 1. An Aspiring Young Jazz Musician

> I was as moved by the recordings of the humpback whales
> as I had been the first time I heard Charlie Parker and
> other great jazz players. Their voice was sort of a cross be-
> tween an elephant trumpeting and Miles Davis. They had
> this bluesy quality that was so poignant.
>
> — *Paul Winter to David Rothenberg*

When Winter was a teenager, he discovered in jazz many
qualities — emotionalism, sometimes exuberant, sometimes
reflective — that he later attributed to whale songs. He had
developed a childhood reputation as a clarinetist in the small
city of Altoona, Pennsylvania. A failed audition as a drummer when he was in first grade led to two parallel tracks of
lessons, classical piano music with "a wonderful old-fash-
ioned teacher named Alma Leighty" and an eclectic approach to clarinet "with an equally wonderful teacher named
John Monti." Since the local newspapers, the Altoona Tribune and the Altoona Mirror, reported on an ongoing basis,
Winter developed a reputation as a soloist with ongoing
achievements in playing a clarinet and other instruments. In
tenth grade, he was the piano soloist for George Gershwin's
*Rhapsody in Blue*. Meanwhile, a new instrument began to
command his attention:

> I became really intrigued with saxophone, I looked for-
> ward to that so much, and finally, I guess when I was

seven or eight, they got me a sax — I first loved the clarinet, which is a close cousin to the sax. But I loved the sax more.

In 1957, his senior year, the high school band premiered his original composition for saxophone and band titled *Soliloquy in Jazz*. Winter's teacher John Monti "had experience with jazz. He'd play jazz licks and bluesy things and I'd love it." Winter said, "For all the years I was in Altoona, until I was 17, I had these two teachers, these two musical streams — kind of the Apollonian and Dionysian sides of the music." Both sides, the emotive with Monti, and the mannered with Leighty, would continue to remain aspects of Paul Winter's musical identity. Winter identified with the jazz personalities that he read about in *Down Beat* magazine, among them trumpeter Clifford Brown and pianist Richie Powell, whose fatal auto accident occurred not far from Winter's home town.

The young Winter's greatest love was not the role of soloist, but the experience of being a member of a band or orchestra. He said:

> I loved playing, but I didn't like the role of being the wonderful young boy all the older ladies made a big fuss about. I didn't want to be the star. What I came to love more, what gave me a path where I exercised my musical enthusiasms, was being in bands.

Winter's first professional experience came at age 17, joining the pit orchestra for a musical that toured Midwestern state fairs. His fellow musicians included members of the Ringing

Brothers Circus touring band. His musical tastes evolved as jazz transitioned from the big bands of Glenn Miller, Benny Goodman, and Guy Lombardo during the 1940s to the small ensembles of the 1950s. A number of important bands performed in nearby Carrolltown, Pennsylvania. Winter continued to love the big band music of Stan Kenton, but, increasingly, it was "the great small groups of that decade: Dave Brubeck, Gerry Mulligan, the Jazztet, Miles Davis ' Kind of Blue Sextet." Thinking back, he said:

> We went to these clubs and heard Miles with Trane, Horace Silver, Gerry Mulligan, Stan Getz, and the guys who lived in Chicago, Gene Ammons and Sonny Stitt. That was a real halcyon era in jazz.

Winter learned about the latest music at Chicago clubs during college at Northwestern University, a short distance north of the city. "... the south side of Chicago was just roaring with bebop. I spent most of my nights driving from Evanston on the north side of Chicago down to the south side, hanging out in jazz clubs. I was just enthralled with that music." His guide was fellow student, trumpeter Dick Whitsell, a protégé of Freddie Hubbard. Winter tells it:

> Whitsell had grown up on the far south side of the city in what was a genteel residential area. Going to Chicago was my first encounter with another culture as opposed to the white one with which I had grown up. But to come into the south side of Chicago, where I spent a great deal of time, and to have a guide like Dick Whitsell, who through his teens had hung out in the black community, I couldn't call it dumb luck but maybe smart luck. That community

was so welcoming... in the era of jazz on the south side. It was a wonderful time and, of course, I was new to a lot of the music and new to the culture. I was just very lucky to have had that much access to the music and to this community of musicians.

Winter formed the Winter Jazz Sextet in college, featuring Whitsell, soon joined by baritone saxophonist Les Rout, and a crack rhythm section including pianist Warren Bernhardt, bassist Richard Evans, and drummer Harold Jones. Evans had been an early member of the Sun Ra Arkestra. Jones played with Count Basie, and was an accompanist to singer Sarah Vaughn.

By 1960, the Sextet's music emulated the harmonically rich sounds, spacious solos, and blues-inflection of Miles Davis's *Kind of Blue* (1959, with saxophonists John Coltrane and Cannonball Adderley), Benny Golson and Art Farmer's *Meet the Jazztet* (1960), and Jimmy Heath Sextet's *The Thumper* (1960). The instrumentation, featuring a three-horn frontline — trumpet, alto and baritone saxophones — was modeled upon those bands. Winter also loved Stan Kenton's lush big band arrangements, and the rich sonorities of Gil Evans, particularly on Miles Davis' *Miles Ahead* (1957), *Porgy and Bess* (1958), and *Sketches of Spain* (1960). A number of Winter Sextet's arrangements were purchased from Jimmy Heath:

> ... we came to New York and were trying to find Jimmy Heath. We eventually found out that he was in Philadelphia, and went there, and found him, at his mother's house. He was staying there at his mother's house and he

was so touched that people had driven all the way from Chicago to look him up. And we wanted to see if we could buy arrangements from him. He sold me the very charts, the very parts he had used on these records, for I think something like $10 a chart, something unbelievable. I remember we got seven charts and it was $70, and I think I had to call my father or something to get the money. That was a real big deal in those days. Jimmy was extraordinarily generous with us... So we had Jimmy's charts and we had some other very good jazz charts.

In 1961, the band won first place in the Intercollegiate Jazz Festival, at Georgetown University. The victory, in May of Winter's senior year, came as a surprise, although the band had placed second a month prior in the Notre Dame Collegiate Jazz Festival. The competition was, most fortuitously, judged jointly by iconic trumpeter Dizzy Gillespie and record producer John Hammond. The prize was a record contract with Columbia Records, for which Hammond worked. That outcome changed the calculus of the young saxophonist's thinking about his life, at least for the moment. He had planned to attend law school, but:

> This was beyond our wildest dreams! Most of us had made plans for grad school, but we all decided to take a year off to 'try this music thing'... I had a lucky break. There were no young musicians making their own records.

Even with a contract, life as a jazz musician was not easy. The musical economy was, as it remains, highly competitive, and opportunities, particularly for relative unknowns are limited. The major pipeline of opportunity for a young musician like Winter would be a track record of touring and re-cording with a big-name musician. Band leader Paul Winter was an unknown college student, albeit hiring notable play-ers.

> During that summer I stayed in Chicago and my band ma-tes and I were trying to find a way to get some work. Even though we had won the festival, there were very few jazz groups getting work. We did have to promise that later in the year we would make this jazz record for Columbia.

The band played fraternity, sorority, and Naval officer club dances: "we would play straight jazz and get away with it..." To call the ensemble a "college" band understates its level of musicianship, as Winter notes, "I had some of the best young jazz players in Chicago."

Over the next two years, the membership of the group shifted to include such luminaries as drummers Fred-die Waits and Ben Riley, and bassists Bob Cranshaw, Chuck Israels, Cecil McBee, and, for one evening on The Tonight Show, Ron Carter. The band was able to book two more fes-tival performances that summer, in Evansville, Indiana (where the Dave Brubeck Quartet and Duke Ellington were also on the schedule) and Saugatuck, Michigan. The first of the band's recordings for Columbia was made in December 1961. But no obvious breakthrough moment seemed to be on the horizon:

> ... that summer I was of course unemployed. I mean get-ting work was sort of like a distant dream of any jazz mu-sician. It was hard enough for the great and famous jazz

players, but for fledgling players to get work... We played
dances and played as much jazz as we could get away with,
and that's how we kept alive, both musically and other-
wise.

The logjam was broken when Winter decided to contact the
United States State Department "and see if they would con-
sider sending us on a good will tour," as they had with Benny
Goodman (to Russia) and Louis Armstrong (to Africa).

We thought our touring might really resonate with the values they were exploring and putting forth... The idea was
to send the top college group in the nation to universities
in other countries.

In retrospect, it seems implausible that two college students,
even with solid bandmates, a competition prize, and a record
contract so far unfulfilled — it would be released later in
1961 as *The Paul Winter Sextet* — would be invited to front for
the State Department. Yet this was the era of the Kennedy
Administration, whose newly founded Peace Corps sent
young Americans to teach and engage in community support
projects around the world. The Sextet's model of racial coop-
eration, comprised of equal numbers of black and white musicians during the height of the Civil Rights Movement and
the Cold War was a plus.

In August 1961, with the help of professors at Northwestern, Winter drafted a proposed itinerary and submitted
it as part of their pitch. He drew upon contacts he had previ-
ously made across Cold War Eastern Europe and promised
that each foreign university visit would include concerts,

workshops and other "offstage activities that the famous groups would rarely do."

The State Department indeed wrote back, requesting an audition tape, for which Winter borrowed $70 to record. After hearing it, the band received an affirmative answer, but not for a tour of Eastern Europe. Winter tells us:

> We got a letter back in October and they said they were going to send us to Latin America for six months. This was a total 'pulled out of the heavens' experience. We were kind of floored. I mean to get six months' steady work and to go to all these countries, it was a great, great stroke of good luck. In January of 1962 we left for Haiti, shortly after a December recording session, thereby fulfilling Columbia Records 'promised contract. We began a tour of twenty-three countries in Latin America. We played over a hundred and sixty concerts in sixty-one cities. It actually changed our lives. It was so fantastic. We were very well received.

The music was welcomed and no doubt provided a goodwill gesture for the U.S. government. Unfortunately, however, little activity followed upon the band's return in July. No acknowledgement came from the State Department, and domestic performance opportunities failed to materialize. A promised Birdland show fell through. Record sales were slow, as Columbia failed to release the first album in the United States or Europe. Although *Jazz Meets the Bossa Nova* (1962) was on its way, riding the Brazilian music wave, following Stan Getz's *Jazz Samba* (1962) with guitarist Charlie Byrd, Winter recalls: "that was the end of the band."

Except, once again, Winter made another gutsy pro-active move. He had written President John F. Kennedy during the tour about their positive experiences: "I told him it was a good idea for them to send out student groups on these cultural exchange trips." His letter elicited an invitation from first lady Jacqueline Kennedy for the band to play in the East Room of the White House, a first ever for a jazz group. The appearance was part of a "Concerts For Young People By Young People" performance series. Voluminous press attention arose from the event, helping to propel Winter's career. He recalls: "'Jackie Digs Jazz! ' On the strength of that we got our first cross-country tour of jazz clubs."

Portions of that concert are documented on the album *Jazz Premiere: Washington* (1963). A subsequent American tour of colleges, with new band-members baritone saxophonist Jay Cameron, bassist Arthur Harper, and drummer Ben Riley was documented on the recording *New Jazz on Campus (1963)*.

Yet once again, the band hit a dead end in 1963, after recording its final album, *Jazz Meets the Folk Song* (1963). The record date emerged from an invitation by producer John Hammond to attend a Pete Seeger concert at Carnegie Hall. Hammond was tracking the growing market for American folk music (particularly Bob Dylan), and he sought to engage the saxophonist's interest. Cecil McBee was now the band's bassist and his arrangement of *We Shall Overcome* appears on the album. But Columbia dropped the Sextet from its label due to poor sales, and Winter turned the page. Ironically, thirty-three years later, Winter served as recordist and producer of Seeger's recording *Pete* in Winter's barn.

Paul Winter's immediate future included a period of self-discovery in Brazil, a musical culture he first experienced while on State Department tour. In Brazil, he gained a new-found love of sounds and rhythms softer than the jazz he knew. Still, the sound of the jazz saxophone and trumpet, and the repetition and variation of melodic patterns within jazz, came to mind when Winter heard the humpback whales. He described them as: "singing long, complicated patterns that sometimes were a half-hour in length, and then they would repeat the whole complex song again, almost verbatim."

Despite edging away from the aesthetics of jazz, the soloist style, harmonic language, and driving rhythms, Winter retained its sounds deeply within his subconscious. It is no wonder that Winter's first experience of hearing songs of a different species, the humpback whale, might have evoked an association with jazz.

## 2. Exploring Musical Brazil

> The great thing about music is the actual playing, the physical vibrations of playing music. Composing music is fine, but I'm speaking of the actual playing. The actual vibratory experience of making sounds and sharing that with other people is so renewing and nourishing that I often like to suggest that people look to the music itself for some of the answers. If your spirit is awakened and alive, you can deal with a lot of realities and problem solving. If your spirit is discouraged, then those things can be pretty daunting.
>
> — *Paul Winter*

Winter's choice to major in English during college, rather than music, may have set the tone for what he describes as his "lifelong protest against the academic aspects of music." As he put it, "I didn't want to study the kinds of things they studied in music school. But I didn't know what else I wanted to do." He planned to become a lawyer, but" music was simply a fervent avocation — something that I'd always done." He said: "There was never any thought that I was going to be a musician. Music was just something you did, like physics and Boy Scouts and 50 other things. I thought I'd be a lawyer." But even as an English major, music remained at his core. He was eloquent: "I didn't give a damn about academics. Northwestern was near Chicago, where I could hear jazz."

Still, while playing steadily through college, it didn't occur to Winter to make music a "life path." As his Sextet gained notice, an acceptance at University of Virginia Law School awaited. Yet an early childhood experience at a Shriner dance had an enduring impact:

> Watching the drummer, Henry Hammond, doing all these things with his hands and his feet. I was blown away. I remember the feeling at those events, the feeling that where music was played was where people had a good time. I think that's motivated me all my life.

And if music were to play a part in his goal, to engage in something "important" and "worthwhile," Winter would have to conceptualize music-making in a way that was different from his previous experience and of a kind that he had yet to imagine.

Among his past experiences were his elementary school period "The Little German Band" (clarinet, cornet, trombone and tuba), which played "oom-pah music and told jokes"; a Dixieland group; the Silver Liners dance band; experiences at the Culver Military Academy where "I got to ride horses and play jazz. It was heaven"; or even in the Paul Winter Sextet, his award-winning college-era hard bop band. During a year a year in Brazil towards the end of his Sextet's run (he would return for two more stays, the final one in 1965–1966), Winter found himself seeking new avenues for expression.

Internally, Winter was rebelling against the jazz traditions he knew and played, particularly bebop and hard bop.

On various occasions during the late 1980s-1990, Winter recalled his misgivings about jazz as he had experienced it:

> We played some jazz clubs in those days, and I remember sometimes turning around and looking at this drummer, a great, wonderful drummer, but he was just banging away on the cymbal incessantly, just ding, ding-a-ding, ding-a-ding, ding-a-ding, ding-a-ding, and I began to wonder, Why the hell is he hitting that thing? Why do we do that.
>
> In all the bop years, all the music I loved was loud. We even played ballads loud. In Brazil, it was like I was discovering the feminine dimension in my life for the first time. I fell in love with the classical guitar.
>
> I found that playing loud and strident alto sax was not a complete expression of my esthetic. I wanted also to be able to play quietly, and I wanted to be able to play with a control that might make it appropriate to play Bach on the saxophone. And I wanted a different approach to percussion, with a completely wide-open door to all the percussion in the world. I heard other percussion in Brazil which I loved very much ...

In Brazil, Winter discovered the music of Heitor Villa-Lobos and deepened his appreciation of Brazilian songwriters Carlos Lyra, Luis Bonfa, Antonio Carlos Jobim, and Joao Gilberto. Brazil became "musically my second home." What struck Winter the most about the new music he discovered, bossa nova, was the way it embodied "the same commitment to beautiful melodies and lovely harmonies that were integral to the big band era. These were just great songs but with a very different flavor. It was rhythmically beguiling in a very gentle way."

For Winter, this was "gentle music that also had soul." He loved the instrumentation, guitar and soft, lilting rhythms. This instrumentation began to find its way into Winter's music towards the end of the Paul Winter Sextet, when departing trumpeter Dick Whitsell and pianist Warren Bernhardt were replaced with flutist Jeremy Steig and a classical guitarist. Visits to Brazil resulted in two Brazilian-influenced albums: *The Sound of Ipanema* (1964, featuring songs by Carlos Lyra, with Sergio Mendes on piano) and *Rio* (1965; songs by Roberto Menescal, Luiz Eca, and Luiz Bonfa).

Upon his return to the United States, Winter formed the Paul Winter Brazilian Consort. The band consisted of Winter's alto sax, plus guitar, bass, a drummer from Argentina, and alto flute, a lower pitched, broad sounding cousin of the standard flute. After listening to the music of Heitor Villa-Lobos, particularly *Bachianas Brasileiras, Number 5* for cellos and soprano, Winter wondered if the cello could play a central role in his music. Could cello be combined with the guitar? Winter was a horn player and he loved horn arrangements, but could the horns be replaced by a form of "gentler horns?" What kind of horn might that be? Winter remembers a moment when he first considered the possibility of English horn, and an aesthetic differing from jazz:

> When I was about 21 or 22, I was halfway through our State Department tour of 23 countries, and I think it was in Ecuador, up in the mountains, at the home of the cultural attache of the U.S. Embassy in whatever city we were in. He played me a recording of a piece called *The Winter's Passed* by a composer from Eastman named Wayne Barlow. It has a beautiful lyrical kind of Americana melody, and it

features English horn, with I think strings, small orchestra. And it was so moving to me. It touched me. There was something very poignant about it. It was that it wasn't loud, and it wasn't bebop. There was the root of a classical aesthetic in me, from all the music I'd heard as a kid: all the symphonic music, and I'd played in a symphony in Altoona, lots of orchestra music, and 12 years of piano lessons. I'd heard Bach every Sunday in church.

Oboe and English horn were familiar instruments, but could they span musical styles? These were horns that could play crystal clear contrapuntal lines, and phrases that weave like jazz lines. Were there double reed players who could play with the freedom and expressiveness of a jazz musician?

What about the sound of his own saxophone? Winter liked the vocal quality of saxophonists Stan Getz and Paul Desmond. Getz was an example of a saxophonist who was playing samba and bossa nova. But he wanted to sound like himself, not imitate other saxophonists. If an instrument in his ensemble was to sound like the human voice, it would be the cello. Winter turned to the soprano sax for a bit in 1963, yet continued to play alto saxophone even after starting the Consort. In 1971, he returned to the soprano, which he found projected better than the alto, particularly when playing outdoors. By the end of the 1980s, the saxophone sound he was aiming for was "a dark, fat sound ... with vibrato you can turn on whenever you want, in any degree you want, but a sound that has strength and life in it just on straight-tones."

What form might the drumming take if it were to differ from jazz ensemble kits: quieter, complex yet simpler in their sonic presentation? In 1966, Winter tried out combining "a jar drum from Israel, a lot of the different wonderful African drums... these big surdo drums from Brazil." Paul Winter spoke of his music as "a forum for all the musics that I loved." What kind of ensemble could accommodate his new, broader musical palate, with roots not only in jazz, but spanning European classical music, particularly Bach, Villa Lobos, bossa nova, and Brazilian popular song?

The instrumentation and rhythms of bossa nova would remain central to Winter's aesthetic in future years, and the soprano saxophone, cello, and double reeds (oboe and English horn) would prove to be excellent choices of instruments to imitate and emulate the sounds of wolves and whales. In brief though, "it was the influence of Brazil that was at the root of the Consort."

## 3. Consorts!

> I borrowed the name 'Consort' from the ensembles of
> Shakespeare's time, the house bands of the Elizabethan
> theater, which adventurously blended woodwinds, strings
> and percussion.
>
> — *Paul Winter*

In 1968, Paul Winter conceived of a musical ensemble modeled upon the England Elizabethan-era" consort." This concept proved compelling due to its diversity of instrumentation, musical forms, and mixture of composition and improvisation. Winter had been in search of a format outside of jazz that could accommodate the wealth of ideas he wished to synthesize, melding both sides of his early musical education in Altoona, Pennsylvania, the "Apollonian and Dionysian sides of the music." The Consort eventually became the vehicle for much of Winter's subsequent music.

In a 1977 interview with Elizabeth F. von Bergen, Winter described his goal as "consort music for the enjoyment of everyone," and not just the audience (as in symphonic music) or the players (as per chamber music). David Darling recalls that Paul explained clearly that the word "consort" means "miscellaneous musicians play miscellaneous music." Winter described it slightly differently during a concert at the Amazing Grace Café, Evanston, Illinois, May 31, 1975:

The definition of 'consort' ... being the name used for the first instrumental ensembles with specific orchestration. It evolved during Shakespeare's time, the house orchestra for the Shakespearean theater. They were unique groups in several ways; particularly that they tried to blend woodwinds, strings, and percussion into it, with a certain organic sound. Also, within each piece they allowed the players the freedom to embellish. And so, modeling this group after that in certain ways, we've also wanted to follow another aspect of the early Consort, the Elizabethan consorts, which is that any of the groups could be combined in any pairing or any threesome of the players or instruments within the consort, and make still a smaller one. The simplest definition we have for consort then is 'conversation.'

In his program notes for a 1982 concert at Princeton University, Winter adds more details:

Born of the theatre, the original consorts evolved first as playhouse ensembles for the traveling drama troupes of Shakespeare's time. Basing their compositions on the popular tunes, marches, folk dances, lute airs, and madrigals of the Elizabethan Age, they developed a new instrumental art form, using techniques of improvisation and free embellishment. They were, in a sense, the jazz bands of Shakespeare's day... If chamber music is more for the private pleasure of the players, and symphonic music more for the public pleasure of the listeners, then 'Consort Music 'is a wedding of the best of both worlds. Music which turns-on the players and is for the enjoyment of a wide audience.

The core members of the original Consort included cellist

Richard Bock, bassist John Beal, English hornist Gene Murrow, and flutist Virgil Scott. The band recorded *The Winter Consort* (1968). By their second album, *Something in the Wind* (1969), Paul McCandless had replaced Gene Murrow. On both recordings, guitarist Gene Bertoncini was joined by Lutenist Karl Herreshoff. The Consort's original percussionist Ruth Ben-Zvi, playing non-Western drums, was replaced by drummer Steve Booker.

Improvisation was an important aspect of the band's music making. Paul Winter recalls: "In the early days of the Consort we never rehearsed. We never had a place to rehearse, so we experimented on stage. I've always regarded the Consort as a garden in which you plant seeds — all these instruments and new pieces, seeds of melodies and rhythms — and see what grows." As Consort tours began to include musical exploration workshops at high schools (Winter preferred not to use the term improvisation), the Consort's inclusive spirit and freedom to experiment extended to musical amateurs. "When they begin to consort, they discover that they're capable of creating a beautiful interweaving of free-flowing sound."

The malleable concept of the Consort proved suitable for the integration of musical aesthetics, styles, and cultures, and the combination of improvisational and through-composed music that would interest Winter in coming years.

## 4. A New Consort: *Road*, and *Icarus*

When David Darling plays, the music's going along and he plays just one note. That's not necessarily 'David the virtuoso'; it's that the music was going along one way and then 'the cello comes in! 'And he makes that life-changing.

— *Jim Scott*

*David Darling in Performance, "8 String Religion," circa 2001*

After *Something in the Wind*, Paul Winter reconstituted the band. Next to be hired as part of the rebuilding effort was guitarist/pianist Ralph Towner.

Paul Winter had heard Towner playing at a New York club. Piano had been Towner's first instrument, followed by trumpet. He turned to the classical guitar only in his senior year of college, and then travelled to pursue it further by studying in Vienna with Karl Scheit. He said, "I practiced 9 to 10 hours a day, 7 days a week for a year. At the end of the year I could play classical concerts." Towner was becoming a solid guitarist, and after his return to the United States, he became increasingly influenced by Brazilian music, "especially Jobim's writing," he said. He toured briefly in 1970 with Brazilian singer Astrud Gilberto's trio. After moving to New York City, he said that "half the set would be jazz piano and the other half, on classical guitar, would be bossa nova and I might play one classical piece."

Winter told Towner that he also needed a bassist and percussionist. Towner suggested two friends: Glen Moore and Collin Walcott. Towner and Moore had been friends in college. Moore's first instrument was the piano, taking up bass at age 13. He began performing the next year with the Young Oregonians (from Portland, Oregon), along with saxophonist Jim Pepper. It was at the University of Oregon, where he majored in history and literature, that Moore learned about the great jazz bassists Ray Brown and Charles Mingus. He studied bass formally after college.

Glen Moore recalls: "In 1964 I drove from Eugene, Oregon, to the Vanguard in NYC to hear the Bill Evans trio with bassist Gary Peacock who was in his bullfighter period... After graduation I spent six months in Copenhagen studying the recordings of Paul Bley with Steve Swallow and Gary Peacock, listening nightly to the great young bassist Niels-Henning Orsted Pederson at the Montmartre Jazz House where I was able to sit in with Dexter Gordon, Ben Webster and Stuff Smith, to mention a few." His career continued in New York City, performing with Paul Bley, Annette Peacock, Jeremy Steig, and Warren Bernhardt.

Towner and Moore had first met in 1959. They became a jazz duo. When they began to play New York City clubs, their music was modeled upon the interactional style of Bill Evans and Scott LaFaro.

Collin Walcott met Glen Moore in New York City, and Moore introduced him to Ralph Towner. The three of them backed folk singer Tim Hardin at the Woodstock Festival in 1969. Collin Walcott brought to the Paul Winter Consort a synthetic approach that engaged Indian and Western musical traditions. Walcott had been a student of Ravi Shankar and Alla Rakha, masters, respectively, of the sitar and tabla. He also performed as a classical percussionist in several symphony orchestras. In a 1981 interview, Walcott recalled:

> I graduated from Indiana in '66, and I went out to L.A. I came back to New York in '67, which was right about when the Indian craze was happening. I already knew something about it, and I could read Western music. A lot

of the people who got into Indian music were hippies and spiritual trippers who were into it more for the experience than for the music.

He encountered Ravi Shankar at a musical instrument store in New York City, House of Musical Traditions. Walcott continued:

> The store's managers got in touch with Ravi's managers to see if they could set up a situation where Alla Rakha would teach a tabla class in the store once a week. The store also gave my name to Ravi's managers as somebody who knew Western notation and Eastern notation so I could help him transcribe examples for a book he was going to write about Indian Music. After I had graduated from Indiana, I studied ethnomusicology at UCLA so I had learned Indian notation. That's how I met Ravi, and then later they said. 'Would you mind driving him to the airport?' Maybe he liked my driving, because the next week they said. 'Ravi wants you to go on the road with him. 'That was a couple of years, traveling around as Ravi Shankar's road manager... I spent most of the time studying with Alla Rakha... so I really had more actual instruction on the tabla than I ever had on the sitar.

Towner takes up the narrative: "The three of us joined the Paul Winter Consort in January of 1970 and there we met Paul McCandless, who was already part of the Consort." Glen Moore recalls that they were hired by Winter "for a fifty-concert tour — at last playing on a big stage with an adult sound system." The Paul Winter Consort was now: Paul Winter, soprano saxophone; Ralph Towner, guitar; Paul

McCandless, reeds; Glen Moore, bass; and Collin Walcott, sitar and percussion, which included a snare drum, a bass drum, a hi-hat, and some cymbals. Cellist Richard Bock was only occasionally available to perform with the Consort, so Paul Winter still needed a cellist... until he discovered David Darling. Or rather, David Darling discovered him.

David Darling was raised in a strong musical environment in Elkhart, Indiana. As a young pianist, he developed a love of improvisation. Much to his family's relief, he learned to read music while studying cello in public school. Darling played piano in blues bands throughout his early schooling and he aspired to become a jazz pianist. Yet there were obstacles: He was inclined to play more freely than was the norm in conventional settings; and it was his father's strong desire that he complete his college degrees and build a career as an educator.

After completing a master's degree in Music Education, following his father's wishes, Darling began a doctoral program in cello at the University of Indiana at Bloomington. But he left Bloomington to teach secondary school, following which he joined the faculty at Bowling Green University in Lexington, Kentucky, in large part because his skill at solo free improvisation had captured the imagination of the interview committee. And unlike many faculty who left Lexington and moved to Nashville to build studio recording careers, Darling promised his new department chair that he'd never leave. But his phone rang during the first spring semester. It was Paul Winter looking for him.

Darling had attended a concert by the Paul Winter Sextet in the early 1960s during college. A few years later, he noticed announcements on the Bowling Green campus for a show by the newly founded Paul Winter Consort. Darling said:

> I was very surprised that I didn't see cellist Richard Bock's picture on the poster that they had put up around campus, because that's the cellist I knew had recorded with the Consort, the great Richard Bock. Paul Winter was sitting by himself after the concert, so I just went over to him and said: 'I love your group. Can I give you my name, and could I audition for your group sometime?' He seemed a little bit stunned and said, 'sure.' I didn't know at the time that many cellists had put out the word that it was a really terrible gig because it was all whole notes and there was nothing hard to do.

Sometime after that first conversation, Paul Winter called, inviting him to sub on a gig. As Darling describes it:

> Paul said: 'I'm sure you're too busy, but I'm calling you because I'm looking for a cellist for a gig in Deland, Florida.' He had never heard me play and, as he told me later, my name was the last note in the last pile of cello notes that he had. He saw my name there, and he called. Since I said I was a faculty cellist, he figured if I could hold the cello, everything would be ok. So, I went down and rehearsed with this group — I didn't know any of them, but they all turned out to be unbelievable people. Ralph Towner, Paul McCandless, Glen Moore, and Collin Walcott. I subbed on the gig, and then Paul said after the concert, 'I'd love for you to do this full-time, if you'd like to.' I said yes and flew down.
>
> I'll never forget the first time I played. In those days of

the Consort, the routine was that the band played the first half together and at intermission, the cellist always came out and played something by himself. All the cellists before me, including the great Richard Bock came out and played unaccompanied Kodaly or Bach. I went out, playing my ass off, improvising. I made something up. Ralph Towner, offstage, said to me, 'what in the fuck was that? That was unbelievable. I never heard that piece!' So, I got more encouragement to just do it. I always thought the classical idioms were so cliché in a way. The idioms were clearly identifiable whether it be romanticism or impressionistic or avant-garde or whatever. So, that's how the whole thing started for me.

That one-time opportunity led Winter to welcome Darling as a full member of the Consort. Darling remembers:

When I first joined the Consort, I basically felt intimidated. They had all been with Paul for a couple years, and Glenn and Ralph had known each other since college in Oregon. I just couldn't believe I was given the chance to play with these guys. Because every night I got to hear them play, and I was going 'Oh, my God.' I mean, just to hear Ralph play every night play a free solo is like an amazing education. Because, you know, he would blow everybody's mind, whatever he made up. What Paul McCandless, one of the original improvisers on the oboe, could do with the oboe and the English horn were off the scale. And then Collin Walcott was the sweetest guy; and the first American sitar player who ever made a reputation. He was a protégé of Ravi Shankar, and for a while Shankar's road manager. He was so gifted as a human being. If it weren't for Collin I don't think the group would have lasted for very long, because the egos were so big, and Collin managed to get everybody's personalities satisfied. He was a such a kind man; he wouldn't let things get out of control. He would step in, say something, and then we'd coalesce to what Collin suggested. I just thought I was living in heaven; when I was a kid, I thought maybe someday I'll be in a band, and that happened to me. It was an incredible experience that definitely changed my life forever. I learned so many musical things from the guys in the band.

The new Consort initially continued the eclectic approach of its predecessor, but things soon changed due to the compositional spark of guitarist Ralph Towner. Paul McCandless recalls:

Paul Winter was very consciously trying to integrate the grooves from all of the great music traditions and wound up getting kind of stuck until the point that Ralph broke into the group and started blowing out this music.

Towner adds:

When we joined Paul Winter he was playing everything from Elizabethan music to Brazilian music to adaptations of baroque music and some adaptations of Bartok. He was playing a collection of styles rather than an amalgamation of styles... what happened was this unusual instrumentation triggered my composition mechanism again, which had been sort of dormant since college, since I'd graduated, and I started writing original material for that group.

David Darling expands on the nature of the group:

There were written charts for every tune. The charts for everything were basically pretty simple. There were no music stands. The music had to be memorized as quick as you could. In my second year with the Consort, Ralph Towner wrote the famous tune, *Icarus*. He came up to me five minutes before the concert started and said: 'Today I just wrote this tune. 'I did get it right the first time. The band never had any bad nights. The distinct sound of the Consort was because of Paul's saxophone. Everything was built on him being the lead player all the time. So, there was a set sound to most everything, even though we began playing Ralph's music.

Permission to improvise was welcome in the Winter Consort. We always did a piece that, in a way, changed my view of music. Paul would say, 'ladies and gentlemen, we are going to turn the lights off, so you can't see the musicians. We want you to listen to the sounds we were making. 'That provided a piece. There was a lot of room for improvisation in different pieces, like *Ballad in 7/8*. That was a chart to just set up the cello player to play a solo. And that's another reason why for years and years, I played that tune, so every night I got a chance to wail away on whatever I wanted to do. That's eight years of concert after concert, getting to be as free as I wanted to be. I mean, it was like a gift from heaven, in a way like 'wow! ' Years later, I took the improvisational idea and made my own company called *Music for People*, based upon four people sitting together and making up music.

The Consort's tours were built around the college circuit. Ralph Towner reminisces about the tours that are documented on the 1970 recording, *Road* (1970):

We had been traveling for seven weeks all over the United States. We finally arrived in Los Angeles where we had set up a soundstage just to play our repertoire for producer Phil Ramone. He was a more pop-oriented producer, but famous for his sound quality. He agreed to record but he didn't know who wrote what pieces. We started playing a lot of pieces by Paul Winter (not really written as much as suggested), and we also played all of my pieces that we had in our repertoire. Phil Ramone ended up selecting just my pieces, and a few arrangements that Paul Winter did... I think he recorded some live concerts, but only one tune was recorded in the studio and that was *Icarus*. Phil Ramone said that it was going to be the hit tune, so he wanted to do it perfectly in the studio. We did that when we got back home in New York City, and we did it in one take... We're really proud of *Road*, I still think that first one is the best version of *Icarus*.

*Road* became one of the recordings that was carried aboard the 1971 Apollo 15 moon mission. Winter comments:

> That was quite an honor. The astronaut in charge of the mission in Houston was the brother-in-law of our cellist David Darling. He liked our music and turned the astronauts on to it, so they took it with them.

To record *Icarus* (1972), the second Consort's sole studio album, Paul Winter wanted to find a quiet, informal, unhurried, unpressurized atmosphere. Winter found what he was seeking by renting a house later known as Sea Weed Studios, located by the Atlantic Ocean in Marblehead, Massachusetts. Winter said: "That landmark experience underscored the importance of establishing a place where we could nourish our music and our community."

Winter invited producer George Martin (of Beatles fame) to oversee the album. Paul McCandless recalls:

> Paul Winter was dying to work with George Martin because Paul was looking to find the most powerful, smartest producer he could to help get his music, and instrumental music in general, out to the wider public. George's signature was putting all these unique-sounding instrumental breaks on the Beatles records. They weren't the normal guitar solos: sometimes there was a string quartet or a Salvation Army brass band or you name it... Some of the solos on *Icarus* were overdubbed, like Ralph Towner taking a solo on a Renaissance Regal, which is a very ducky little reed organ. A lot of times, we were in the same room and could see each other when recording. It's not the way you do it nowadays. George did a lot in terms of getting the takes that we needed. He was tireless that way... He brought a really high level of performance to it that we weren't used to.

The instrumentation for the recording was unusually diverse, as George Martin notes:

> The whole group had all sorts of percussion instruments — amadindas and xylophones and gourds and things — which would fill the back of a truck. So it was ethnic music, and yet it wasn't; it was folk music, as well. It was near classical music, too.

Paul McCandless:

> I had this gigantic sarrusophone, which is a bass reed in-
> strument, like an octave below a baritone sax. On this one
> piece, we used it to *double* some of the bass lines, and it
> gave a tremendous impact. It put a real edge on it. You
> couldn't really hear it; you just heard that the bass had got-
> ten more potent... I remember there was one piece for
> which we were looking for a big tamboura sound. George
> had the whole band come out, and we held down a chord
> and the middle pedal of the piano, which effectively cre-
> ates a harp. Then he had the band strum the piano, and
> they recorded it but with the tape turned around so they
> were recording it backwards. So there was this big cre-
> scendo, and the engineer, Bill Price, faded it before it actu-
> ally hit the attack. It had the effect of this swarming,
> swirling kind of thing.

Capitol Records initially funded the production for $65,000
but pulled out of the deal. Winter signed a contract for its release on Epic Records, which in turn dropped Winter from
its list of artists due to limited sales of 25,000 in its first year.
Ironically, *Icarus* continued to sell, by the mid-1970s totaling
200,000 copies.

## 5. Playfulness and Musical Creativity

There needs to be a place, a space (even for a weekend, or a minute) where each person is totally all right, just as they are, right then and there... where whatever they do, play, or say, is all right... is totally fine. For maybe this can enable/evoke a break-through, an experience of freedom... or self-acceptance... or connectedness... a place of grace, we might say... that can stay in the body-memory. Even when you return to the old familiar contexts you might remember this experience: 'I soared, 'or 'I felt at home, 'or 'I felt good about me. 'To have an epiphany like this, even for a moment, is a triumph.

— *Paul Winter, following a 2010 workshop*

*Paul Winter and Eugene Friesen from a concert on April 10, 2017 at Congregation Beth Shalom Rodfe Zedek in Chester, CT. Photo by Deborah Rutty.*

A serendipitous experience expanded Paul Winter's musical conception. The Winter Consort's eponymous first album (1968) includes a four-and-a-quarter minute free improvisation titled *Koto Piece (Free Improvisation On A Koto Scale)*. The melodic material for this rudimentary improvisation included the notes on the strings of a Japanese koto that Paul Stookey gave Winter. Although Paul Winter and flutist Virgil Scott were experienced improvisers, two of the four group's members were not. Cellist Richard Bock and English hornist Gene Murrow were classical players.

The piece opened the door to Winter's practice of including a free improvisation on concert programs, played with stage and house lights turned low. By the 1970 tour, the Consort consisted of the deeply experienced improvisers, Ralph Towner, Collin Walcott, Paul McCandless, Glen Moore, and David Darling. On the Consort's album Road, the fully improvised track is titled *Come to Your Senses*, the name Winter gave to this series of collective improvisations.

David Darling's successor as Consort cellist, Eugene Friesen, prefers the term "spontaneous composition." Friesen explains this usage: "We use that to give dignity to our better improvisations when they seem to transcend noodling and riffing, and when we're working with thematic material."

Winter's interest in guiding young musicians to "come to their senses" was kindled by an invitation to offer master classes by the Consort at the Hartt School of Music in

Hartford, Connecticut in 1971. It was highly unusual to encourage free musical exploration in a conservatory setting, but the experience opened the door to a template Winter would begin to develop.

David Darling narrates:

> Paul started doing workshops in the 1970s. It was a package deal. He began offering, instead of just a concert, a concert and a workshop. When he was invited back to places where he had given concerts, there would be a workshop for people who wanted to learn more about improvising. I enjoyed working with him and being part of it. I've always had a knack for being an effective teacher. I was just assisting. I'd help get things organized from time to time, get people in the right quartets; make sure that the experienced players realize that, with your experience, you should be able to help everybody, not showing off.

Darling discovered something new through this process:

> One of my approaches to life, as it turned out, is the fact that free improvisation was more interesting to me than organized improvisation. Actually, as I grew into everything, I didn't want to study anything. I liked freedom."

When Darling began to lead his own workshops, he found that

> piano players who were classically trained, it blew their mind when they found that they could improvise. It wasn't that big a deal. There were so many variations people could get into, in terms of what they were imitating.

Susan Osborn, who would later join the Paul Winter Consort, attended a 1975 workshop. She describes Darling's role as being more substantial than Darling himself modestly recounts it:

> Our Osborn's all-female musical group Garden went to the 1975 workshop. David Darling primarily facilitated, and it was utterly life changing. He approached music from a similar place as we were. Playing music was about relationship and being vitally alive, expressing that aliveness in sound, in musical expression. Even at that point, in 1975, I recognized something in the music, wow, you know, this is extraordinary. And the same with David and Paul as teachers. It was profound.

Winter was uncomfortable with the term "improvisation," which for him evokes an over emphasis on virtuosic display and a rehashing/imitation of favorite "licks" that sometimes characterizes idiomatic jazz performance practice. Winter was far more interested in helping musicians unlock their innate expressiveness, their ability to use their instruments and voices as vehicles for self-discovery. If anything, what Winter developed was an antidote to conventional master classes:

> There are often inhibitions associated with playing music, and I like to overcome those as quickly as possible. So in the workshops I suggest a moratorium on 'loaded 'words — like 'improvisation' and 'talent'. Instead of the word 'improvise 'I sometimes suggest the word 'noodle'. You may not think you've ever improvised, but most everyone has noodled around at one time or another, when you were

next to an instrument (such as a piano.) But the more dignified term I like is 'sound-play'. Each of us has a well-developed instinct for spontaneity which we use all of our speaking lives. In sound-play we are simply using the language of sounds.

The goal was not to teach skilled musicians how to more adeptly play notated classical music, nor is it mastery of the bebop idiom with ornate arpeggiated swirling lines of its great soloists, beginning with Charlie Parker and Dizzy Gillespie. If anything, Winter desired "to take all those wonderful musicians and create different contexts for them where they'd get to have a more personal voice. My fantasy is to divide up a symphony into twenty or thirty different consorts, of all different instruments, and scatter them about the floor of a large arena. And the audience would get to sit on Persian rugs scattered about, wherever they wanted, among the ensembles."

Winter hoped that experienced musicians could use their instruments as an extension of their inner selves. He articulates this idea in a 1990 interview:

The power of aliveness is the most precious thing. That if you can find what sparks that aliveness in you, whether it's picking the horn up and finding one note that you love or playing something you love, or playing with other instruments that you love, that's the thing to keep alive. Technique and all that is useless if there isn't that love in it.

Paul Winter's interests began to shift away from working specifically with skilled musicians, and more towards people from all walks of life, of all (or no) musical backgrounds. The goal became to awaken people's playful selves, their child-like potential to let their hair down using sound: "Spirit comes alive most universally in nature and in shared experiences with other people and through expression. Giving out is the fulfilling thing — not taking in..."

People would sing and play, freely making sound in small groups, seated in a darkened room. The goal was to listen closely, rather than look at one another, leave behind concerns about musical notation or preconceptions, critical evaluation or judgment.

In 1977, Winter invited people to join him in Baja, California, for days of whale watching and music making. He coined the term "Adventures in Sound Play," which remains the title of his workshops:

> All we'd do all day is make music and watch whales, and the effect of being in that environment was extraordinary. People started coming out of their respective closets and freely expressing their songs, their stories, their dreams, their struggles, everything. It was as if everyone became like children, unfettered in their singing of the song of their life. It was clear to me that nature was a place for opening up these expressions. It's not about virtuosity. It's about tapping the basic instincts for expression everyone has. Humans have an abundance of it, but most of us don't use it because you got clamped shut in the fourth grade when somebody said you didn't have talent. Or maybe you were scared and said it to yourself. It's amazing how much expression is blunted in our society.

Paul Winter's workshops during the late 1970s included week-long "Living Music Village" encampments at his Connecticut farm. Advertisements for these workshops stated: "No Musical Experience is Required."

The workshops continued at retreat centers, among them The Esalen Institute, Kripalu Center for Yoga and Health, Omega Institute, Rowe Conference Center, Lama Foundation, at colleges, and at one point, at Jane Fonda's ranch. During the early 1980s, each of the members of the Consort would lead their own workshops and come together to give Consort performances. Guitarist/singer Jim Scott recalls giving a workshop at Rhode Island College when he first joined the group. Paul Winter continues to describe the workshops he leads in this way:

> The Adventures in SoundPlay Workshop offers you the experience and tools to enable you to make your own music, grow your own pieces, create your own 'bands', and for you to BE as music in your life, resonant with your world, confident of the song that is you. The process strengthens your appetite for adventure in life and gives you confidence to pursue your dreams. It awakens a quality of aliveness to ourselves and our environment. We humans refer to states of heightened awareness as 'peak experiences', a label that implies how infrequently we know this condition of full aliveness. In music-making, it is possible to reach this state quickly and sustain it.

While Winter's workshops have been dedicated to musical free play, David Darling came to shape the concept in a more structured format, paying attention to a core set of concepts about making music. These would later be codified as, as Darling recalls:

> a musical 'Bill of Rights 'that says very succinctly that all sounds go together, and enjoy dissonance when you have it. I had observed what Paul did. I adopted some of that but not all of it, because when I started doing my own stuff, I wanted to do it in another way.

Susan Osborn titled her voice workshops "Seeds of Singing" and "Singing for Everyone." Osborn describes her goal for participants:

> I want them to go into 'my life depends on this. My life depends on me making this sound. 'What I'm really interested in is the sound before any concerns about pitch or rhythm, or any of that. I'm concerned about the basic sound coming out of your soul. Now, for a lot of technically trained people, this is totally antithetical to everything they've studied, everything they've been trying to do, which is to get a handle on that wild horse. I've got to get a rein on this thing, put up the corral, we went don't want this thing running wild. Without access to your soul, without access to that tiger that lives inside you, it's just some beautiful sound. It's so difficult. And I know this from my own experience. It's difficult to allow ourselves to be that un-composed. To speak the unspeakable.

## 6. Electric Winter

> When Paul Winter and his Consort came to Vermillion South Dakota in 1975, it was a marvelous version of the group that never released a recording. They came to do a concert and workshop. The Consort concert was mind blowing.
>
> — *Susan Osborn*

*Susan Osborn. Photo by Melanie Flint*

By the time the first Consort ended in 1973, most everyone was ready to move on. The four members who would become known as the band Oregon were already functioning as a unit when they entered the Consort. They sought a higher level of musical complexity and interaction than they found with the Consort. David Darling acknowledges:

Consort fans began to understand that Oregon was really quite something. They were really playing instrumental music that was in a sense even more sophisticated than Paul Winter's music. To play in that band required, you know, higher musicianship. They were heavily endowed with jazz musicians, some of them writing charts. Still having in it English horn, oboe, and the guitar kept it in that Renaissance kind of thing.

Some band members were frustrated with Winter's environmentalism. Tension had developed between Ralph Towner and Paul Winter, although Towner recalls: "We came away from that tour with the Consort with a great experience having put a lot of written music out so that we were ready to go on our own."

While on tour with Winter, in June 1970, Oregon recorded their own first album *Our First Record* (unreleased until 1980), and subsequently recorded *Music of Another Present Era* (1972). For Glen Moore, the time with Paul Winter provided "an encouraging circumstance to be able to play music that we enjoyed playing on a stage." He continues: "We'd been doing it prior to that time in bars and stinky little places. So the experience with Paul Winter was a really good one and launched us in a way, introduced Ralph to the 12-string guitar and introduced us to Paul McCandless."

As one Consort came to an end, a new one came into being. This more electrified band toured most heavily in 1975, never releasing an album, and provided a transition into Paul Winter's more overtly environmentally oriented bands. David Darling continued to perform with Winter until 1982. Darling recalls:

> The group, that second generation of the Paul Winter Consort, we were tight. We toured the college circuit (although Paul began to travel separate from the rest of the band) and we did some recording. The group never recorded an album, I guess, because it just never was the right time. It's an interesting question, because we sounded great in that group, too.

Susan Osborn, at the time a singer in Garden, a woman's trio, recalls Winter's band during that time:

> A giant circle of timpani and Brazilian marching drums was drummer Ben Carriel's territory; Tigger Benford, tabla; Robert Chappell, keyboards; David Darling, cello; and Paul Winter, sax. The music was electric, and a new combination of classical and jazz sounds. It was something about the fierceness with which this band played, and the refinement at the same time that moved me profoundly.

Winter remembers it a bit differently:

> We briefly tried an electric fling in the mid-seventies, and I put pickups on both saxes and I had speakers behind me, and we had a whole little sort of Emerson, Lake and Palmer type of ensemble with our own tractor trailer, six tons of gear, an electronic organ, and all of things. The cello was electrified, and we did that for a minute, you know, for about a year.

The climax for Winter was experiencing his horn physically breaking:

> One night out in the Midwest in some gig I finished playing the soprano, and I laid it on top of the amplifier, which was quite high, it was up on some risers, and I went to get the alto and I tripped over the cord, and yanked the soprano down, and it landed on the side of the riser, and got twisted into a pretzel.

Fortunately, Winter's saxophone repair person in New York City was able to fix it. In sense, this experience seemed to be a metaphor for Winter's situation at the time. For him, the Consort was ending, and he was undergoing a shift towards a different kind of musical life: "My life was getting too complex. The whole idea of keeping a band alive and well in the world and traveling all the time and records and dealing with all the questions; it's a rather crazy existence." Most immediately it meant choosing just one of his three soprano saxophones to serve as the instrument he'd master. But more broadly, it pointed towards centering his life and musical creativity at the farm he had purchased in Litchfield, Connecticut.

In 1976, Paul Winter founded the Living Music Foundation. Its purpose was "exploring and implementing ways in which music can be used to enrich the lives of human beings, and awaken a spirit of involvement in the preservation of wildlife and the natural environments of the Earth." By the next year, he was in a boat off Baja California playing to gray whales.

Meanwhile, Osborn, after studying at the University of South Dakota, toured that state for six years, playing rock and roll in bar bands. At the time when she met Winter, Osborn had formed Garden, with Colleen Crangle and Marilyn Wetzler Castilaw:

> One time while traveling west, Paul was driving and came through Vermillion. I needed to get to the other side of the state, for a gig at a bar in Spearfish in the Black Hills, so he gave me a ride across South Dakota, which at that time was an eight-hour trip. We really connected, sharing songs and musical ideas and bits of our history. That was probably 1976. The next year, I was living in a little tiny town of 11 people outside Vermillion, Spink, South Dakota. And my house burned down, in January, to the ground. That was kind of the first sign that I was cosmically being booted out of my little life in South Dakota.

Osborn joined and was quickly fired from a country swing band, and then "I got a letter from Paul, inviting me to come to Connecticut and stay on his farm to record *Common Ground* (1977) with him and a group of musicians he had met along the way. The beginning of a new life."

That was the summer of the Music Village. Susan Osborn continues:

> Later the following summer of 1977, I traveled from the Black Hills to Litchfield, Connecticut, and lived in a tent village on Paul's land with 30 other musicians. We wrote together the lyrics and music and recorded in Paul's barn. An amazing group of people from all over. The process of creating that music echoed the title *Common Ground*. One

lunch break, Paul pulled a small paper from his pocket, with a note about the song *Lay Down Your Burden* (a song by Garden). Oscar Castro Neves was still in the loft, and Paul asked me to show him the changes for the song. He was sitting on the organ bench and so I showed him the basic chords. After a very short while he had it, and Paul suggested we record it just for fun. David Green, the engineer, was still down in the remote recording truck. We did one take and that was it. David Darling later created and overdubbed with Paul a beautiful arrangement. That recording and song have had a remarkable life of their own and altered the course of my life again.

Paul invited me to join the Common Ground Tour the next year, so I made a permanent move east. When I was not playing with the Consort, I was couch-surfing and apartment-sitting in NYC. I hung out in the Village music scene, playing on the street and working as a folksinger in the clubs, the Bitter End, Folk City, Kenny's Castaways.

## 7. Consort Anew

I learned from Susan Osborn and David Darling that you leave it all out on the floor, give 110% and make it 'bigger than life'… by being real, transparent, vulnerable, authentic… cultivate that balance, that flow, that immersion into undistracted brain and body working. I am happiest when I achieve that.

— *Jim Scott*

Jim Scott's work with the Paul Winter Consort began as an arranger during the post-production of *Common Ground*. Scott had trained as a percussionist, shifting to classical guitar during his studies at the Eastman School of Music. He played an eclectic repertoire in bars. At the suggestion of a schoolmate, drummer Steve Gadd, Scott joined the Army Field Band Studio Band (now called the Jazz Ambassadors). Scott continues:

We went on the road in a kind of scenic-cruiser bus and we had our own little life. I was very lucky to get with such great players; Steve Gadd was the drummer, and Joel De-Bartolo the bass player; Joel later was in the Tonight Show Band for 20-some years. I really wasn't at the level of those guys, and it was trial by fire. We evolved towards playing a lot of current rock tunes, going to high schools and destroying discipline for the day — we are the Army band! Kids would go nuts. Especially when Steve Gadd would start "Get Ready" by The Temptations.

After Gadd departed, Scott took over the drum chair for a time. After Scott himself left the Army band, he performed around the Washington, D.C., area with fellow former servicemen. Scott then headed to the Berklee School of Music in Boston to further his guitar studies. In his words:

> I always felt slightly odd at Berklee, coming from my classical musical background... you know 800, pick-style guitar players! But oddly, all my jazz stuff had been street learning before that... My classical technique and my jazz playing were really like different worlds. I didn't use the classical guitar on gigs. I played electric. I would sometimes play the steel string guitar with my fingers. The whole world of folk finger-picking, I knew nothing about that.

Jim Scott's perspective about the guitar and improvisation would soon change:

> When I first arrived at Berklee, in a snowstorm in January '77, somebody told me that Paul Winter had just played there, and they had a posting on the bulletin board that Paul Winter was looking for new players for the band. So, I thought, 'Well you know, here I am, back at school. Maybe just sending an audition tape is a good exercise.' So, I made an audition tape, playing a classical thing, and a jazz thing. I talked to his manager and she said, 'well, you know, we got 100 tapes already. The soundman's going through them, but you can send one if you want.'

The audition tape never went anywhere, but as Scott prepared to return to school for another semester and had just taken a room in a group house in Boston, the phone rang.

His roommate called out: "Paul Winter's on the telephone for you!" Scott tells the story:

> I answered the phone, and it was Gene Bertoncini, who had played with Paul Winter long before. He said, 'Hey, Jim, I'm in the studio here with Paul Winter, and we were talking about you and I was telling him you're just the guy for him. You play classical and jazz, and I wonder, would you want to meet Paul Winter? 'Winter got on the phone and said: 'I hear you do a lot of arranging. We've done a lot of recording on this album, *Common Ground*, and we need some arranging. Would you be interested in coming in, looking at the arranging things?'

Scott traveled to Winter's farm after the conclusion of that summer's Music Village. While helping clear some brush from recently downed trees upon his arrival, the thought came to Scott: "This is what I want to be involved with, this kind of music, and this environmental message." Winter gave Scott some tunes that the band had recorded, "and I went home and wrote a bit of an arrangement, adding cello, English horn, and sax background to the first song, and then to a second." The simply chordal arrangements weren't appealing to Winter, Paul McCandless, and the others. Scott describes it:

> What Paul really wanted me to write was free flowing lines that were more contrapuntal, which sounded like separate personalities, things just easing in and out. I did another round and I think I caught the idea. One important value was 'less is more' — half of what I wrote was actually enough. After I did that a couple of times, I saw what they were looking for and the beauty of it. This has informed

my life ever since. It was a good lesson.

Scott became the singer on the title track *Common Ground*, and arranged and expanded upon Winter's song melody and David Darling's chords to *Wolf Eyes*. Secure in his knowledge of the sound Paul Winter was aiming for, Scott arranged Susan Osborn and Garden's song *Lay Down Your Burden*, for doubled saxophone, oboe, cello, and a pump organ chordal drone. Later that year, 1977, Scott formally joined the Consort as its guitarist and he continued to compose and arrange for the Consort. Among his work was a harmonization and expansion of themes from the sea mammal song that became *Lullaby for the Mother Whale* on *Callings* (1980). Scott describes what emerged:

> This sequence sounded almost like a Bach progression; it is just eight bars, round and round. And then I threw in a bridge. The new group had become a really tight band, going on long touring trips, but just scraping by financially... And then the Consort settled into Nancy Rumble playing English horn and some keyboards, and then Eugene Friesen, playing cello. With the Consort, I played the 12-string guitar and a classical guitar. That became the group that we had for the next five to seven years.

In addition to Paul Winter on soprano sax, this core group also included Paul Halley on piano and organ and cellist Eugene Friesen. Various percussionists, particularly Ted Moore and Glenn Velez, served in the Consort during the early 1980s. This was the band that participated in Winter's musical adventures along the Colorado River through the Grand Canyon. Nancy Rumbel proved to be just one of two female instrumentalists to serve as regular members of Winter's Consorts. Flutist Rhonda Larson was the other. Other women were vocal soloists, and Ruth Ben-Zvi, a percussionist who played with the group in the 1960s.

*Eugene Friesen, Solstice Concert NYC, 2019*

Eugene Friesen joined the Paul Winter Consort through a chance encounter with Winter that sparked Friesen's interest in improvisation. Winter led an improvisation workshop at Fresno State University in 1973 in which Friesen, an FSU student, participated, before departing to complete his studies at the Yale School of Music. The musical chemistry between Friesen and Winter remained on Winter's mind. Five years later, in search of a replacement for David Darling. Winter invited Friesen to join the Consort, where he has remained ever since, touring the world, rafting the Colorado River, and performing in the annual Winter Solstice events.

Growing up in a musical family, Friesen's father, a university choral director, essentially assigned the cello to become his son's instrument. Ever since, "the cello has been my lifelong companion." Trained as an instrumentalist in Western notated music traditions, he built his career primarily as an improvisor, as Friesen terms it, "an improvisational cellist." As he explains, his music emerges from listening closely to the subconscious:

> And we can access, with a certain kind of stillness and kind of musical preparation... a lot of the music that I've birthed has been really just the product of my curiosity and my affection for some sounds, some rhythmic feels, some chord progression you know that I've stumbled on over the years.

In addition to his work with Paul Winter, Friesen has had an active career as a solo cellist, and taught strings, for the past decade at the Berklee College of Music. His musical inspiration continues to span Bach and Villa-Lobos to field recordings of African and Middle Eastern musical traditions, sounds, and rhythms. He has a particularly deep appreciation for the influence of

> Afrological stream of music ... forms that are really much more conducive to improvising than a lot of the kind of through-composed forms from Western music. But the thing that Jazz has really taught us, is how rich our music can be if we really pick from a lot of different streams.

The Brazilian flavor of some of the Consort's music appealed to Jim Scott, who had as a young man been influenced, like Paul Winter, by the flowering of bossa nova, its melodies, chords, and, particularly, the Brazilian rhythms. Scott's words:

> Ted Moore... had lived in Brazil a couple years and knew the samba thing. Paul brought in various Brazilian percussionists as guests in the '80s and for me, that was a great experience, 'I'm playing with a real samba guy.'
>
> The Consort had a particular style of playing. You'd write something that would be the structure or the outline of the thing, but if I gave Eugene Friesen a scale and arpeggio or even a musical line of his own that I had written down for him, he would probably do something different with it; the result would be something else. Nancy Rumble would just take what I wrote relatively freely. It was really a jazz interpretation of music. Paul would want this somewhat composed organization, but he had a 'disregard' for the written parts. When other people try to copy the Consort — they'll play with a couple harmonics in there or some little atmospherics — they miss the point.

The Consort sought a balance between improvisation and a more consistent, composed-sound music ("a bit of the classical side he was trying to come up with"), yet, as Scott notes,

"Winter would be happy if it ended up slightly different," more improvised. Like Winter, Scott emerged out of being a more conventional jazz player rooted in bebop. He remarks that Paul "can really play some stuff! what he calls 'doodle'!" Scott learned a new way of playing from the Consort:

> I would even just observe how Paul McCandless and David Darling and then Nancy Rumbel and Eugene Friesen moved into this same realm. They didn't know bebop licks; they didn't know that you are 'supposed' to play a steady stream of eighth notes or something. They would listen to each other and talk to each other.

Singer Susan Osborn, who had toured with the band prior to Scott's arrival, joined them on a fifteen-show month-long tour in the spring of 1978, returning later for *Missa Gaia* (1982) and other special projects. Scott's assessment of Osborn: "When she opens her mouth to sing, time stops, and this is it." David Darling adds: "Susan is so spectacular, with this usual voice." Susan Osborn reacts to her experience:

> The combination of my voice with those sounds of the Consort was just heavenly, you know, really unbelievable. And it's the brilliance of Paul, once again, choosing my voice, the actual tonality of my voice, with David's cello, and later with Eugene's cello, with Paul Halley on piano and Cathedral organ, with Nancy Rumbel's instrumentation, and of course with soprano sax. How all those tonalities blended together. They were made for each other. I was classically trained vocally, so I have this voice that was also tempered in bars, you know, it's a very unusual kind of sound. I felt completely and utterly supported by every musician that I worked with in that group. I think they felt

I too was supportive of them. It was a very harmonious collection of people.

There were so many transcendent musical moments with the Paul Winter Consort... It was brilliant. It was arrangements, the sensibility, not only Paul, but Paul Halley, and all the players, really. There is a video of the Consort in an outdoor concert in 1983, and I'm singing *Lay Down Your Burden*. It is a strange and wondrous experience for me to look back on my thirty-two, thirty-three year-old self, and see and hear who I was and who I was privileged to make music with. These incredible musicians — Oscar's in it, and Jim and Ted Moore's playing percussion, and Gordy Johnson's playing bass. It's just so beautiful. And I would say that video exemplifies my experience of the school of being in the Consort. And Paul always said it was a school, and it was a school for sure.

The band with Jim Scott remained together consistently until about 1984. They engaged in numerous projects, generated by Paul Winter's broad vision and by invitations that came his way, often supported with limited funding. One such event was a gathering of international communities, among them, for example, Paulo Solari's *Arcosanti*, north of Phoenix, Arizona. The gathering took place at the Findhorn Foundation in Scotland.

*Winter and wolf*

## 8. Winter and Wolves

> It's a profoundly nourishing and transforming experience
> to be in nature without fear. If we can overcome the fear of
> these creatures, maybe it can encourage us to overcome
> other fears – even the things we fear in ourselves.
>
> — *Paul Winter*

While Paul Winter was speaking of the human fear of
whales, he was also thinking of wolves, one of the most his-
torically stigmatized animals on the planet, as in the apho-
rism "a wolf in sheep's clothing."

Pam Brown, aka Many Stories Wolf, has for many
years coordinated grassroots educational efforts about
wolves. She carries on the work of the late John "Wolfman"
Harris, who was well known for bringing *ambassador wolves*
(wolves born in captivity) to schools and public events, "pro-
moting the animals as an endangered species."

Brown explained that Harris "first learned about
wolves in the 1960s when his wife, who ran an animal sanc-
tuary, brought home a wolf puppy she'd gotten from an ex-
otic animal dealer." Brown tells this story:

> The two would sometimes chain the young to a tree in the
> yard. One day their landlord came by and asked if their
> 'dog' was eating his chickens. It seemed impossible that
> the wolf, named Rascal, could be the culprit... One day he

observed Rascal tip over her dish, and then, with her nose, scatter the bits of kibble as far as the circumference of her rope would allow. Then she lay down and appeared to doze. Soon, a couple of chickens came clucking by, pecking at the chow. Rascal then sprang to life, pounced on the chickens, and broke both of their necks. In no time, Rascal devoured her preferred meal of fresh meat, feathers and all.

John Harris developed a rapport with wolves and came to a nuanced understanding of their character. He learned how prevalent were negative stereotypes of wolves, perpetuating fear and leading to their near extinction. During the late 1960s, Harris began to travel with Clem and Jethro, two ambassador wolves; these were among the fifteen ambassadors Harris worked with over two decades.

In 1968, Paul Winter attended one of Harris's early programs at a middle school in Redding, Connecticut, close to Winter's home. Winter was fascinated with these animals. Hearing their howl, he was struck by their gentle sound. Winter and Harris became friends and visited each other's homes. A few years later, in 1973, biologist Fred Harrington introduced Winter to wolves living in the wilds of Minnesota. Researcher David Mech, author of the foundational 1970 study *The Wolf* also served as a guide in Winter's explorations.

Paul Winter's felt connection with wolves guided him to recognize that human beings are part of, not separate from, the natural world. He realized that this awareness had begun early in his life, as it does for children who are exposed to nature.

> We all started out as environmentalists as little kids. I think we were all naturally connected to the earth and its creatures and place a pretty high priority in that, if my four-year-old daughter is any indication.

He continues:

> When I played the tom-tom for the Order of the Arrow ceremony when I was 12 years old, at the Blue Knob Boy Scout Camp outside Altoona, playing that drum in the forest at night, I was thrilled by the sound. That was a place where I felt whole.

The evolution of his mature awareness continued in 1965, when Winter viewed televised footage of seal pups being killed for their coats. His reaction:

> I had felt a terrible helplessness, not knowing what to do. I felt the same frustration three years later when I learned about the whales... but by then I was finally moving towards using their music.

The Paul Winter Consort first performed a musical composition on the theme of endangered species in 1970. *In Wildness is the Preservation of the Wild* was a new work for instrumental music, narration, and the sounds of wild animals, inspired by a Sierra Club book of photographs by Eliot Porter, with text by Henry David Thoreau. Winter remembers:

> The piece was a kind of requiem and it took me a while to realize I wasn't going to do a whole lot of good for the

earth by making people feel guilty. The job of shocking people with the grim facts is for other media — film, or the press, or literature, or painting. The best job that music can do is to celebrate the beauty and the glory of wildlife and the Earth... I had to find a way to express my feelings about this new, larger home I had been ushered into by the whales, in my own medium, which is instrumental music. I came to realize that celebrating the beauty of the living creatures was a more effective strategy to move people than depicting the horror. The best way to raise awareness about the magic of the vocalizations was to find a vocalization we could interplay with, so the actual voices of the creatures were woven in with the music. In a sense we were collaborating with these creatures.

In search of "a single, easy term that would define animal sounds coming from wild places," naturalist/musician Bernie Krause invented the term *biophony* to identify the sounds created by animals in specific environments. One might say that Paul Winter's musical aesthetic is to interweave sounds of biophony with the sounds of musical instruments.

A few years after meeting John Harris and his wolves Clem and Jethro in the mid-1970s, Winter was introduced to Ida, a wolf living in captivity. Her voice would be heard on Winter's song *Wolf Eyes* included in *Common Ground*. David Darling explains how this came about:

> What started our using animal calls was Paul wanting to have a piece that honored the wolves, their howling that he thought was just fantastic to hear. He was looking for a composition, and it ended up that he used a composition of mine, except with his melody. This was after Ralph

> Towner and company had left the band. I wrote that music and he put his own melody to it, and that's the famous wolf call. I later put that on a record of my own that I call *Minor Blue*, with my own melody. Paul Winter, on the basic recording of *Wolf Eyes* is so close in pitch and melody to the first wolf call that when you hear him, it's almost verbatim the same lick.

Jim Scott remembers how the melody was built upon the wolf call motif with chord changes by David Darling. "Paul had picked some pre-recorded wolf howls, and determined that the howl was sort of in D-flat or B-flat minor." Scott revised David Darling's initial chord changes and added in some development, a crescendo coming to a climax. He then added a cello line, following Winter's instructions for it to be akin to *Icarus* but in a minor-key. Scott selected phrases from a variety of improvisations that Winter had recorded, and these became the saxophone part. Paul Winter commented that "we credit the wolf as the co-composer."

Winter's soprano saxophone proved to be a natural choice to emulate a timber wolf call. Their sounds seemed sonically related, as would the sounds of humpback whales and cello, as played by David Darling, and later, Eugene Friesen. John Schaefer, host of the Public Radio show *New Sounds* observes:

> Paul was the first to make animal voices part of his ensemble, in the same way human instruments are. Some see Winter as a kind of musical shaman, a shape-shifter who can make his own instrument sound almost feral. A timber wolf, a Weddell seal, even a killer whale, many of whose calls, he points out, 'are naturally within the top range of the sax.'

*Wolf Eyes*, however, was not music of wolves, but rather, of humans, drawing upon wolf motifs. It was the result of an unfolding, multi-stage human compositional process. Initial ideas were proposed, selected, and deleted. The form emerged from a process of experimentation and editing before arriving at a final version. The process of composition that resulted in the final version was quite different in kind from the howls of wolves. Winter comments:

> Before we play the piece, *Wolf Eyes*, I talk about what the wolf howl means to them. The wolf howl reaffirms their 'togetherness' as a pack. It's not meant to be scary or anything. This is a lesson that we might learn from them. At the end of the piece, I invited the whole audience to join us in a 'howlelujah' chorus...

During the concert tour of music from *Common Ground*, Paul Winter periodically incorporated an actual wolf named Slick within his performances. Jim Scott recalls:

> John Harris had raised a couple of wolves in captivity. John was taking the wolves to schools and other places. He befriended Paul Winter. He brought a wolf to a concert at some point, and everybody just loved this. So, I recall that we did it four or five times.

The goal was to educate people about wolves and normalize their presence. Scott continues:

> He was totally gentle; he certainly wasn't going to attack. But he is a wild animal; they don't do anything you tell them. You don't train them to come or anything. But he was so totally fine with people around people, yet couldn't

have lived in the wild. So, I didn't see anything wrong with keeping this guy alive in captivity with humans, though they're not pets.

The decision to bring a wolf onstage made newspaper headlines, including in the New York Times. It also raised questions about how to best balance educational goals with boundaries that protect the needs of wild animals. I personally recall attending the Audubon Society benefit concert at Carnegie Hall, September 8, 1978, and feeling uncomfortable about a leashed wolf standing onstage before a massive audience. David Darling echoes this sentiment: "It's another thing to drag a wolf into an environment that has nothing to do with what is natural." Other members of the band shared these concerns. Susan Osborn: "This was not a domesticated animal by any means. I was the one who had to get the wolf to howl during concerts. I was the wolf whisperer." This was not a role that Osborn liked. "Sometimes, the wolf will look at me like 'you've got to be kidding. Who in the hell are you?'"

### 9. Howling of Wolves, Howling Like Wolves

> I loved the idea of music for the earth. It's music and adoration for the sound the wolves make, what it means on our planet that animals do communicate, and some of them do it in what we would call a musical way. In fact, it's probably true of all species, that they communicate through sound. Someone once told me that they slowed down some bird calls, so it was ten times lower than it should be, and it sounded like whales. And I'm a believer that all sound is music.
>
> — *David Darling*

When Paul Winter asked Roger Payne how he could be helpful to endangered species, Payne told him, as David Rothenberg relates, "to make sure nature has a place in your music." Paul Winter had long strived to engage rather than merely entertain his audiences, and one aspect of this was to familiarize people with the sounds of wild animals, to sensitize people to their presence, and to lessen our fears and increase our appreciation. Winter's goal:

> As soon as we humans discover that animals are not dragons or demons, we want to have conversations with them and relationships with them, the way we have with each other. It's an admirable and ingenious impulse, but there also has to be a voice reminding us that we don't really know what animals are thinking. There's wisdom in mystery.

The collective human "howl'elujah" chorus became a staple

of Consort performances. This idea did not originate with the Paul Winter Consort. Public "wolf-howling programs" have taken place in Canadian National Parks since 1963, beginning in Algonquin Park, Ontario. They became an official part of the interpretive program in Canada in 1972, first in Prince Albert National Park, Saskatchewan, and subsequently elsewhere. A goal of this program has been to bring people out into wolf country and "a means to an end, namely, striving for a better understanding and appreciation of parks systems," while hopefully not disrupting the lives and behavior of the wolf packs. Its planners also hoped that "howling like a wolf" might "stimulate the howling of wild wolves" so that visitors might hear wolf howls.

Wolf howls serve multiple functions in the wild. Researchers Erich Klinghammer and Leslie Laidlaw, building upon David Mech's work, observe that wolves are "either territorial, migrate long distances, or live as loners." He continues:

> In these conditions, an effective communication system between pack members, various packs, and loners has evolved to facilitate or prevent interactions between packs and individual animals. Howling, in addition to scent communication, is one way in which wolves communicate. At times, three or more wolves engage in 'chorus howls,' whether spontaneous or elicited by other howl-released stimuli.

Paul Winter points out that wolves can howl for the sheer joy of it, one starting the song, the others chiming in on different notes." His incorporation of audience participation howling "in a 'howl'elujah chorus'" ritually simulates a sense of being part of a pack, however briefly. Concert goers become participants rather than passive audience members, and ideally experience something of the vocal quality of a wolf's howl. To howl, one reaches deeply into the lungs and cries out, without words or semblance of human culture.

The composition *Wolf Eyes* addresses not the collective nature of wolf howls, but the solo howl of a loner wolf. It speaks to our human relationship to them as individuals. Kinghammer and Laidlaw found that solo howling "prior to and during the first part of the breeding season" can be perceived by people in human emotional terms and consequently are termed the "call of loneliness", although these often occur in the presence of other wolves. The *Wolf Eyes* motif is a solo howl. The harmonic cycle and minor mode of the song suggests a haunting, maybe "call of loneliness" quality.

The combined experience of listening to *Wolf Eyes* and the "howl'elujah chorus" provides a means not only to build environmental awareness, but to encourage people to reach for a wildness with which contemporary music-making has lost touch. Susan Osborn recalls that in the time she spent with Slick, the wolf put her in touch with what it means to "smell wildness. And that is very different than civilization or something being tamed." She implicitly asks what is it that we can learn from wolves, and not just about them:

It touched on an aspect of human experience that has become obscured by our socialization. I think for me I recognized that there was something in me that was untamable. There is a wildness in me that I could kind of touch, and I could experience what I sang, when I went into that thing of singing. It still, it still is there. It's untamable. And I recognize how far away I was from it, too. That I had been tamed pretty well. As a human being, I somehow had been taught pretty well how to fit in and how to manage it. I understood social grace pretty well... this issue of wildness and what does being civilized mean.

Osborn's reflections resonate with this 2014 exchange between David Rothenberg, Dario Martinelli, and Martin Ullrich. Asked by moderator Jessica Ullrich "What can human musicians learn from animals?" Martinelli reflects: "Many things, the most important of which is musically reconnecting with their own animality, something we constantly try to escape from, not only in music." Martin Ullrich responds: "Foremost, singing and listening."

Ultimately, there are limits to what a musical performance can achieve. It is Winter's hope that the power of music to move people emotionally can guide them towards action to protect endangered species:

I've learned that no matter how much information people are given about the plight of endangered species or of the environment, only if they are moved in their hearts are they going to do anything about it.

## 10. Communing with Whales

The natural world demands a response beyond scientific insight. The natural world demands a response that rises from the wild unconscious depths of the human soul.

— *Thomas Berry*

When Paul Winter first heard humpback whale recordings at Roger Payne's 1969 lecture, he discovered not only empathy for sea mammals, but an intimation of the unity of all expressive creatures. He said:

> It made me realize that there is perhaps a universal yearning that is shared by all species, this calling, crying quality in their singing and awakened me to the crisis of what we're doing to the Earth in a way that I had not been aware before. And that became another part of my life's mission. Afterward, I felt as if I had joined this larger fraternity of beings, this bigger symphony of life.

The point would come when Winter would find a way to learn more by experiencing whales "in person." He was struck by the whales' rich timbral variety and nuances in pitch, at times sliding one note to the next. These reminded him of that most prized attribute of great jazz horn players, their distinct sound. And he was reminded of the cyclical melodic patterns used by jazz soloists, complex and abounding in variation — but he hadn't yet experienced whales live in the ocean.

In 1971, a group of activists vowed to peacefully disrupt an American government nuclear test off the Alaskan Aleutian Islands of Amchitka. They boarded a fishing boat named the Phyllis Cormack, renamed Greenpeace, piloted by captain John Cormack. The ship, departing from Vancouver, never reached its destination, but its voyage led to the founding of Greenpeace, the environmental organization.

In late April 1975, Greenpeace initiated a campaign to protect a pod of sperm whales off Vancouver Island from commercial whaling ships. Activists planned to interpose themselves between whales and whalers. Rex Weyler, former Greenpeace director, recalls what was termed The Great Whale Conspiracy:

> We headed up the west coast of Vancouver Island to Winter Harbour, and then out to sea to find whales and whalers. We tested our zodiac skills when we came across wild orcas near Bella Bella in the inside passage.

It was regular practice for Greenpeace members to board small-sized inflatable zodaic boats when whales approached.

A few weeks into the campaign, Greenpeace invited Paul Winter to join the crew as they encountered grey whales in Wickaninnish Bay near a remote fishing village. Winter, as he described it:

> played music to them, and listened for their response. They seemed less interested in us than we were in them, but the whales were clearly curious, bobbing about our little inflatable boats, gazing at us with enormous eyes. The

experience inspired us and provided a story and photographs for the media.

Winter later told David Rothenberg:

> What struck me so deeply was this slow-motion grace, their surfacing, this powerful spout, and then they would dive. Suddenly I understood a whole different aspect, not just this thunderous power.

Winter boarded a zodaic the next day, from which he played saxophone to the gray whales, yet with no discernible response. He narrates another experience playing to orca whales in a boat with orca researcher Dr. Paul Spong off Vancouver Island "during the august weeks when the orcas are most active." Winter tells us:

> Far in the distance we see their blows, like puffs of musket fire from a small brigade. As they come closer diving and surfacing in regular cycles, we maneuver so we'll be in their path. Through hydrophones trailing in the water, we can hear their high-pitched cries... When the orcas are within a few hundred yards, I begin to imitate their calls. This I find fairly easy, since many of their sounds are within the top range of the sax. We guess that the orcas can hear me, since their hearing is so phenomenal, but I have no assurance of this. There are only a few times when it seems like their phrases are imitating or answering mine. But it's of little concern to me. I am thrilled just to be there and to get to play along within the chorus of these magnificent beings...

Late the following year, the Paul Winter Consort performed as part of an official State of California Celebration of the

Whale, and again, in 1977, at Japan Celebrates the Whale & Dolphin — the Seas Must Live. Sponsored by *The Dolphin Project,* the event sought to call attention to the Greenpeace anti-whaling campaign in Japan, a major center of whaling. This would be the first of several trips made by Paul Winter to Japan, some with Roger Payne, to advocate and raise funds for whale protection. When he took part in a 1979 whale watch off the coast of Baja, California, during the making of a film about whales, Winter's perceptions of these animals deepened. He soon substantially devoted his energies towards musical projects about sea mammals: *Callings* (1980) and *Whales Alive* (1987). He described his interaction with the orcas not as communicating, but as communing.

> Communicating I have no idea about; that implies some meaning. I'm no longer interested in what the meaning is. It's enough for me to just be there in the space and commune with sounds... If I'm able to convey to people anything about the wonder of the wild creatures, and about their plight, I think I'll do it with their sounds because it's the closest thing to the spirit of those creatures that you can experience short of being with them...

Ultimately, Winter's response to the whales was two-fold: to simply be present with them, and to compose music about them for a human audience. Winter sought to present the beauty of whale songs and the value of whale life in an accessible way that appealed to human aesthetics. Building empathy for creatures so different from human beings, and so distant from ongoing human experience, requires a bridge of empathy.

Science has increased our understanding of the world of sea mammals, even while viewing strongly that the natural world exists primarily for human use. Human-caused danger to sea mammal habitats increasingly threatens human survival. John Lilly observes:

> Sometimes, I feel that if man could become more involved in some problems of an alien species, he may become less involved with his own egocentric pursuits and deadly competition within his species, and become somehow a better being...

Joan McIntyre optimistically suggests that human beings can perceive greater connection to whales through presentations that are humanly self-referential:

> We are always looking for correspondences. Looking for something that is like us in other creatures. We believe that if we can prove that an animal has human characteristics it is more valuable, more deserving of life... So when we look at whales, when we try to get close to them, or close to what we think they might be, some extraordinary qualities come to our attention.

McIntyre was speaking not of musical presentations per se, but appeals to human-like qualities of the mind of sea mammals. Her words:

> For want of a better concept we call it intelligence, because that's what we think we have. The musical creation and transmission of whale songs, I would argue, is an excellent, even alluring exemplar of intelligence. Music can help us transcend the limitations of rhetoric, however

well-grounded in fact. When we try to discover the consciousness of cetaceans, i.e. sea mammals, through the scientific method alone, we stumble across the problem that
the scientific method seems to forbid playing with its information.

A strength of Paul Winter's compositions based upon whale
songs are indeed his mode of "playing" with a form of musical intelligence that our species share. In his composition
*Sea Wolf*, in *Callings*, Winter draws upon "the two-note call of
the orcas as my seed-theme," grounded in "harmonies in the
C# Major Prelude of Bach, from the Second Book of the
'Well-Tempered Clavier'... The piece is preceded by the orcas
with sax."

Winter's goal shifted from communication with
whales to communication with human beings who have the
collective power to protect our fellow mammals and their
natural habitats. In his estimation: "Music is infinitely flexi-
ble. You can shape it any way you want."

In this case, human music could build upon adapted
whale motifs. The two-note motif accords keenly with Winter's aesthetic of musical simplicity and emotional direct-
ness. Like some contemporary musicians who were educated
in the highly complex and abstract music of the 1940s-1960s,
be it bebop or contemporary art music of the avant-garde,
Winter was among those who began in the 1960s to recon-
sider their musical values. For some, this has meant a new
look at melody and tonality, and for others, a focus on more
accessible emotional and meditative qualities. As sound-
scape composer Darren Copeland writes: "Abstraction closes

doors on the worlds located within the experiential world."

Our present era of unprecedented technological development paradoxically has sparked some, like Paul Winter, to shape their musical skills in a more musically accessible manner, driven by a spirit of wonder in nature and an appreciation of sounds that exist in the natural world.

Maybe Winter's formulation of "communing" is indeed a window into the "spirit of those creatures," conveyed though their sounds, providing a point of shared reference that humans can only intuit in a primal way. Winter suggests that if we cannot gain knowledge of animal music from the perspective of animals, the next best thing we can do is listen with open ears, with curiosity and empathy. The sounds of our fellow species can help stimulate greater human caring for those species and better guarantee their survival on this planet. We can simultaneously broaden our understanding of ourselves, and of the world beyond what we know, from a human perspective.

*Humpback whales, photographed by Wade and Robyn Hughes*

## 11. Celebrating the Music of Whales

> I loved the idea of music for the earth. It's music and ado-
> ration for the sound the wolves make, what it means on
> our planet that animals do communicate, and some of
> them do it in what we would call a musical way. In fact,
> it's probably true of all species, that they communicate
> through sound. Someone once told me that they slowed
> down some bird calls, so it was ten times lower than it
> should be, and it sounded like whales. And I'm a believer
> that all sound is music.
>
> — *David Darling*

As Paul Winter's interest in sea mammals evolved, his music began to express his loyalty to and affection for whales and other endangered species. A goal of his musical world had become championing their inherent right to flourish.

Winter's first musical treatment of sea mammal songs appears in *Ocean Dream*, on the album *Common Ground* (1978). He describes this composition in the liner notes as "a fantasy inspired by experiences I've had playing saxophone to grey whales" during his 1975 and 1979 experiences on the West Coast, set into play by his first hearing of whale songs at Roger Payne's lecture in 1968. *Ocean Dream* is a multi-track sound collage melding human and whale voices, human instruments, and sounds of the sea. It has a slow moving, dream-like hazy texture, often grounded in drones. Among the lyrics to the melody are these words:

> Ocean Child / Come now home / Holy wonder / Wholly one / Ancient song / Call me home / Ave Maris / Ave Om ...

> ... Let me flow without time / Let me rest from my sleep / Let me see in the light / Let me sound in the deep / Let me soar on the silence / Of the Ancient Voice

> ... I am Sea ... I am Sun ... I am Moon ... I am One (Ave Om)"

The poetry evokes a unity between all things, a recognition that life on the planet originated in the sea. The speaker is simultaneously the human singer and the whale. The human aspires to swim with the whales, beyond time, discovering freedom and enlightenment. The whale echoes the most ancient of ancestral voices, the oneness expressed through multiplicity of the sea, the sun, the moon.

"Ave, Maris Stella (Hail, you, star of the ocean)" is a Christian prayer calling upon the mercy of the mother, Virgin Mary. "Ave Om" is a conflation of the Latin "Ave" (Hail) and the Hindu "Om," a sacred sound used in meditation, a way to reference ultimate reality and the inner self. "Ave Om" thus bridges two sacred traditions to invoke the oneness of all things. The singer aspires to merge with the oneness, with the sea as spirit, throughout time, through sun and moon, morning and night.

As the composition begins, we hear the ambient sounds of rushing ocean waters. After ten seconds, a structured whale song appears; at the end of the work, it will return. Each segment includes rising and falling whale motifs.

First, there are two calls and response. Next, the whale varies the rising call and twice-repeats its response: F-F#-G#, closing with C-C#-D-C#. The opening call-and-response is repeated two more times. Paul Winter recalls, in the liner notes to *Common Ground*, the origin of these motifs:

> I wanted to look for a whale melody which we could sing, and see if we could put human words to a whale 'composition.' I found this theme for *Ocean Dream* in a humpback whale song recorded off Bermuda in 1975 by Frank Watlington. The whale sings it in the introduction, and again in the closing duet with the sax. The low whale sounds, at the bottom of the dive, were recorded off Bermuda by the Cousteau Expedition in 1972.

The sung melody opens in this way: the first phrase moves upwards, F-G-B ("Ocean Child"), and returns downwards, C-B-A ("Come now home"), closing with an up-and-down weaving phrase. B-C-C-B ("Holy wonder"), and then down and up, G-E-F ("Wholly one"). A refrain follows. While the sung melody does not exactly reproduce the whale motifs, it is suggestive of its three then four-note phrases, and the upward and downward motion.

Close to the one-minute mark, a human instrumental drone prepares the way for the human vocals, which are joined at two minutes by groupings of whale calls. The whales "add" their voices to an instrumental drone behind the human singer, and then the melody is repeated by the cello. The whale calls vary in range, from high-pitched to slow, downward glissandi. As we approach three minutes, the glissandi slow down and shift steadily lower in pitch. A low-frequency whale motif is heard, followed by the return of the human singer, at four minutes thirty seconds, joined by whale calls. A minute later, the human voices repeat, echoing one another, and they merge with a dense mix of whale songs (Winter describes this as a "'night chorus' from Roger Payne's recordings made in 1970 near Bermuda... ") soon trending towards rising glissandi. The listener is led back, in around five minutes and forty-five seconds, to the ambient ocean sounds, and a return of the opening whale motifs. From six-minutes-and-five-seconds to seven-minutes-and-twenty-seconds, Winter's saxophone imitates each whale call, one after the next; in the background, the vocal melody is played by human instruments. At the end of the piece, all sounds except for the whale motifs and the gentle sea fade away.

As a fantasy, the instrumental drones suggest a timeless quality, as well as the ever-presence of the sea. Whale and human voices sing similar motifs, each in their own accent. Towards the conclusion, a soprano saxophone echoes each whale cry, as if in intimate dialog. The sound of the sea washes over everything, first introducing the composition and then saying farewell.

Paul Winter returned to the theme of sea mammals in *Callings* (1980). In the album program notes, Winter reflects on the opening composition, *Lullaby from the Great Mother Whale for the Baby Seal Pups* and *Magdalena*:

> Listening to a recording of a long humpback whale song I found this melody which sounded like a lullaby. It was

mid-March (1979), and I had just come home from my second Baja California expedition, to read news of the harp seal slaughter that was about to begin in eastern Canada. I was thinking of these seal pups as I played the whale tape... I had this fantasy, that this song, from one of the largest mammals in the sea, was crying out for the fate of these small, helpless creatures. That this really was a lullaby that would resonate through the seas, and surround and protect these newborn pups when the seal-hunters came. It was an act of reverence to put these humble human harmonies beneath this whale melody.

*Lullaby...* was harmonized by Jim Scott, who recalls: "It sounded almost like a Bach progression — this sequence is just eight bars, round and round — and then I added in a bridge." In the arrangement, the cellist plays counter melodies and there is a solo section for saxophone. After the whale motif appears alone, it is repeated while accompanied on guitar by the cyclical harmony. David Rothenberg notes the irony:

> The whales change their song as a population from year to year, so forty years later none of them are singing the same songs anymore. None except for the Paul Winter Consort, that is.

He was referring to the whale song at core of *Lullaby....* The irony is that while the whales themselves may have moved on to other songs, human beings often prefer repetition. The constancy of this particular song over the decades reminds the human listener that "this is a whale I have come to know; every re-hearing calls to mind my connection to the whales." The music is gentle and soothing.

Yet Winter's goal is not simply to calm the listener; it is to sensitize human beings, to soften them for something more than the sake of relaxation:

> ... the aim of my music is not just to make people kind of lay back and meditate, or whatever. We have to wake people up first. And I feel there is much to interest the mind and the mind's ear in our music. It's bringing beauty to people. That's the principal mission, and I think that can have a wakening effect. And/or it can have a calming effect. I'd love it if it had both... But the goal is to wake up, to approach a realization of your true nature as a human being.

During Consort performances, the role of imitating and answering sea mammals was assigned to David Darling and, beginning in 1978, Eugene Friesen. Darling remembers his internal process as an instrumentalist:

> I was really thinking emotionally, intuitively. The whale sound is floating in water, which means it has an expansive quality to it. And when you use an Echoplex, an electronic device that produces an echo effect, you are, all the sudden, in the whale's world... I've always been a lover of space and a lover of rubato and a lover of adagio. During those years, Paul gave me different recordings to listen to, so undoubtedly my ear learned some of the kinds of licks. I tried to find the same intervals and the same pitch the whales were using, and then imitated them by the fact that there's a lot of glissando sounds in whale sounds. And the cello is so easy to glissando.

The listener is scarcely aware of an intentional process behind Darling's whale motifs. Darling's emotional and intuitive process allowed him to respond with musical sincerity as he responded to Paul Winter's devotion to whale song and to the survival of that species. Darling expanded the idea:

> Playing the sounds was also more there than playing a motif, in terms of why that comes out so beautifully. For Paul, he really believes it. He's imitating his friend the whale. And he's doing it because he wants the world to understand that the whales make such beautiful sounds, and that they communicate. His philosophy of life is absolutely inspiring. I've always found his leadership in what he was trying to do to be inspirational. It never, ever occurred to me that it was anything except great.

Winter can assert that "I'm a musician, not a naturalist," yet he represents, as David Darling observes, something far more than a musician with an interest in animals. Winter thinks of whales, and other singing wildlife, as musical colleagues. In the program notes to *Whales Alive* (1987), Winter writes that his first experience in hearing whale songs "opened my ears to the entire symphony of nature." He refers to whales and other sea mammals he's encountered over the years as "musicians of the sea."

The seeds of the recording *Whales Alive* were sewn when Winter and Roger Payne together attended the premiere of the film *Star Trek IV: The Voyage Home* and then proceeded to talk into the night. Payne had consulted on the film; its plot returns the spaceship's crew, through time travel, to San Francisco, 1986, the year of the film's release. The crew's goal was to locate a whale, the only species with which threatening aliens could communicate. Whale song, in this context, represented a vehicle for the survival of the planet.

Similarly, Winter aspires to address the songs of non-human species so that his music, drawing upon animal sounds, might move other human beings to care about endangered animals and habitats, thus perpetuating life on Earth.

*Whales Alive* consists of musical settings of poetry by D. H. Lawrence, Elizabeth Kemf, and Gary Snyder, and passages from *Moby Dick* and Roger Payne's *The Voyage Home*. These alternate with instrumental selections that pair Paul Winter and organist/pianist Paul Halley, and, at times, percussionist Ted Moore, with recordings of whale songs. The album includes additional music from previous Winter whale-themed recordings.

The final track includes a passage from Payne's poem, recited by Star Trek IV actor and director Leonard Nimoy: "Infinite landlessness. I would not trade this hour for anything I know. Rock me gently, ocean, I'm coming home." The narration pauses at two minutes and forty seconds, giving way to a rich pastiche of multi-layered whale songs, joined at three minutes and fifteen seconds by Halley's chorale played on the pipe organ of the Cathedral of Saint John the Divine. Paul Winter adds a melody above Halley's harmony. The instrumental music is a gentle, cyclical musical offering. It doesn't accompany the whales so much as coexist with them. Although the emotionally soothing music takes a more dramatic turn at six minutes and sixteen seconds with the addition of percussion rolls and drum hits, the mutual coexistence of whale and human music is treated a metaphor on this track. It offers hope for the ultimate peaceful cohabitation of this fragile planet by our two species.

The piece, and the recording, closes with the humpback whale motif from *Lullaby from the Great Mother Whale for the Baby Seal Pups*. The reprise of this field recording from the 1970 Payne recording *Songs of the Humpback Whale*, represents a return of the whale songs that first moved Paul Winter.

On *Lullaby...*, from *Callings*, 1980, the whale song was imaginatively interpreted as the mournful lullaby of a mother yearning for her pups. As Winter described it, the call could simultaneously be a cry "for the fate of these small, helpless creatures" and "a lullaby that would resonate through the seas, and surround and protect these newborn pups when the seal-hunters came." *Lullaby...*, and its return on *Whales Alive*, is an expression of empathy and maybe identification with the plight of the whales. It is a song of yearning and hope, projecting the aspiration that whale songs, when presented to human beings in an aesthetically beautiful manner, might shift public awareness about all living things. Maybe it could move a public that seems too often uncaring to no longer standing-by while highly intelligent, conscious animals live or die due to our activities.

Paul Winter's appreciation of sea mammals offers a window into his fascination with the myriad lifeforms of this planet. Curiosity and empathy for endangered species goes hand in hand with a deep care for the environments in which they dwell. These have included the vast expanses of the the oceans, the breadth of the Great Rift Valley spanning the Mideast and East Africa, the reverberant spaces within the Grand Canyon, and the sprawling Colorado River that flows within it. The great scale, as well as the small details of the planet and its environments have long intrigued Paul Winter. So too has he displayed throughout his life a keen fascination with events that traverse great magnitudes of a scale. His Solstice events are the most widely known and appreciated of such events. Yet this concept of scale, and musical spectacle, did not begin with the Cathedral of St. John the Divine, the site of the Paul Winter Solstice concerts. One must look further back in Winter's family history to find their allure.

## 12. Musical Spectacle

Something I learned from Paul Winter and our bandmates,
is that everything can be bigger than life. It's not just that
a bunch of really hip or cool musicians are playing, but it's
going to be a carnival or a circus – a celebration! Paul
would do those kinds of theatrical things, but even if it
was just a band, it was elevated to that rarefied thing the
way the Guarneri String Quartet comes out and we're in
awe. In this case, a bunch of hippies come out on stage
and they're 'the Paul Winter Consort!' Paul would introduce things as, 'Here is one of the greatest musicians I
know' who is going to do a little solo for you, and he would
set it up in a way. With a little hyperbole, he would build
up a concert to be this life-changing experience. People
would come up afterwards and say, 'it changed my life'.

*– Jim Scott*

When Paul Winter was a boy, he recalls, music was "a whole
family heritage... There was lore all around the family."
Among the many musicians in the extended family, Paul
Sr.'s seven cousins comprised the *Noss Jollity Company* vaudeville troupe. Musical spectacle became the business of the
extended Winter family well before Paul Jr.'s birth.

Winter narrates: "... they'd play a whole variety of instruments — seven mandolins, seven trumpets, seven trombones. They played the first saxophones in America, seven of
them, in the 1880s. He continues:

... the family toured in some form or other from 1880 to 1924, early on in a horse-drawn bus. They played six trombones; six herald trumpets which I have, they gave them to me; they played six mandolins; and they played six saxophones, they had the whole family from soprano to bass. I have pictures of them, and my mother has more in Pennsylvania. And I have a lamp in the corner of my living room my mother made out of Uncle Ferd's soprano. You press the E-flat key and it turns on. It's a straight soprano standing up with a shade on it.

Paul Winter was born on August 31, 1939, a third-generation resident of Altoona, Pennsylvania. By the turn of the 20th Century, the population of Altoona reached 40,000 with 15,000 working at Pennsylvania Railroad facilities. The local music store, The Winter Music Store, was founded in the 1880s by Paul Winter's grandfather, Ferdinand Winter. It became the largest in the region. As a teenager, Ferdinand had been a Civil War bandleader on the Union side. Ferdinand's son, Paul Theodore Winter Sr. (September 27, 1887-October 18, 1987) worked in the store as a young man, tuning pianos on the side. He was also a violinist. Eventually, Paul Winter, Sr. and his brother, Arthur E. Winter became proprietors of the store.

Paul Winter's father and grandfather were raised within a musical world of brass bands. It is hard to imagine a town in America, from the mid-19th century through the 1920s, that didn't have a marching band. Emil A. Holz observes: "thousands of bands provided music for parades, civic ceremonials, concerts, and dances."

Bands proliferated across construction plants, towns, and even department stores. As the popularization of movie houses, phonographs in private homes, and competing forms of popular music eroded the staying power of professional bands, wind ensembles increasingly took hold in schools. High school bands were becoming a key aspect of musical education, and musical education was increasingly a fixture within American education. Bands required instruments, thus instrument makers and stores where instruments were sold and repaired were increasingly found throughout American cities and towns. For Paul Winter, growing up in a community-centered, do-it-yourself era helped spawn his musical and cultural values:

> I was simply allured to music as a kid. There was a lot of music in my family and community... It was before mass media, so everybody had to create their own culture locally. I think this was a very wonderful thing. I was fascinated with clarinet and saxophone. I loved bands — especially the big bands of that time. My dream was to have a band at some time.

The composer Charles Ives, a master of musical spectacle, was an attractive model for Paul Winter. This was due in large part to Ives' musical eclecticism, appreciation of songs connected to a sense of place (albeit crafted in highly modernist ways), and youthful memories of brass bands. Ives and Paul Winter's forebears each lived in similar musical worlds. Ives 'lifespan intersected with the two senior Winters: Paul Winter's grandfather was a teenager when Charles Ives was born; Ives was a teenager when Winter's father was born.

Paul Winter fortuitously moved to the home town of Ives, which was Redding, Connecticut, in Fairfield County. Winter's first Connecticut home was in Weston in the mid-60s. Following a brief stay in New York City, he relocated to Redding in 1967, where his bond with the musical legacy of Ives strengthened.

A successful insurance salesman by day and a composer at night, Charles Ives was one of America's most iconoclastic composers, simultaneously worldly and philosophical. His musical work combined rhythmic complexity, tonality that edged towards atonality, simple patriotic American songs, and Christian religious hymns. Throughout much of Ives' music, populist musical forms and references serve complex musical ends. His *Concord Sonata* interweaves a broad range of musical material, from Beethoven to hymns, while his *Fourth Symphony* juxtaposes time signatures, subdivisions of the orchestra (requiring more than one conductor), dramatically contrasting moods and references, texturally dense passages, and an idiosyncratic fugue. It has been said that Ives drew upon childhood memories of his father's marching band performances, during which other bands could be simultaneously playing different music. In his imagination, he heard a complex web of melodic strands, juxtaposed and interpenetrating.

Winter was familiar with Redding, having visited his friend, singer Mary Travers, a long-term town resident. They had met at a 1964 folk-music concert by Peter, Paul and Mary at the University of Tulsa, Oklahoma, which Winter attended thanks to an invitation from Peter Yarrow, the tenor in the group. Winter played a club date the previous evening, and Yarrow came backstage. Folk music was new for Winter, but he enjoyed the show and appreciated the trio's engagement with issues of their time. The two groups then toured together to campaign for Lyndon Johnson. The recording studio premiere for Winter's first Consort was as accompanists for Paul Stookey and Robert Bannard's *The House Song* on Peter, Paul and Mary's 1964 hit *Album 1700*. The Paul Winter Consort's second recording, *Something in the Wind*, was produced in 1969.

In 1974, Winter moved for the summer into a cottage at New Pond Farm, owned by actress Carmen Mathews. Winter recalls:

> It was such a beautiful setting, in the meadow with people looking north. I have a lot of special memories of the farm; it is one of the most beautiful pieces of land I've ever seen. The view from the barn area is breathtaking.

Carmen Mathews subsequently turned the 100-plus acre property into a farm education summer camp for city kids, expanding it, in 1985, as a center opened to the public, as it remains today. After the summer, Paul Winter moved into a house on the same road, Umpawaug Road, where he lived until 1975. As it turns out, Charles Ives had also lived on that road. Winter recalls:

> My time in Redding was a very seminal period for me, when my relationship with nature was deepened, and the Consort was born during that time. It was a wonderful place to live.

Winter assembled a 17-member Consort to celebrate Ives' 100th anniversary, Saturday, August 17, 1974, on the Ives homestead. Winter titled the daylong event "a *Musical Town Meeting*... bales of hay had been placed on the hillside for people to sit on, and we had a truckload of watermelons for intermission." Winter joined James Sinclair, scholar and conductor of Ives' music, in an arrangement of Ives' *Country Band March*. This parody of a small-town band performance proved important in Ives' musical odyssey. He drew upon its musical material to craft *Putnam's Camp*, the second of the works in Ives' *Three Places in New England*. Many years later, in 2009, Winter and Sinclair reprised *Country Band March* on a program that premiered Winter's *Flyways*. Winter describes *Flyways* as "a celebration of the great bird migration from southern Africa up the Rift Valley through the Middle East to Eurasia."

Six years after the *Musical Town Meeting*, the scale and playing field for Winter's musical projects began to grow into far more expansive events. These have included orchestras across the United States: the Indianapolis Symphony, Cape Cod Symphony, and orchestras in Birmingham, Alabama; Cincinnati, Ohio; Omaha, Nebraska; Muncie and Fort Wayne, Indiana; and Springfield, Massachusetts. In Winter's view:

> The live performance of a symphony orchestra offers a wealth of musical nourishment and can act as a bridge to link this gap, the lack of something deeper between mass popular music and the conventional orchestral repertoire, without capitulating to some type of muzak.

The Paul Winter Consort has been joined by the Dimitri Pokroksky Folk Ensemble, Russian *a cappella* singers and dancers; Celtic uilleann pipers; the recorded sounds of humpback whales, timber wolves, and many species of birds; a massive, bell-filled Winter Solstice *Tree of Life*, the *Forces of Nature* African-American dancers, Pletenitsa Balkan Choir. Winter and Consort members have conducted recording sessions in the Grand Canyon; taken a glider trip flying with storks across Israel; and in Russia, traveled to Lake Baykal, and given performances in Irkhutsk and Moscow.

Paul Winter certainly approached his work as a mission, but as he declared to an interviewer in 2000: "Life is always exciting when you view it as an adventure."

[following page]: *The final moment of the 2018 Winter Solstice event at the Cathedral of St. John the Divine, New York. Photo by Joel Chadabe*

## 13. Solstice

> My first experience at the cathedral had been in 1974,
> when I attended the funeral of Duke Ellington. It was one
> of the epiphanic musical events of my life, made all the
> more awesome by the titanic space and acoustics of this
> largest cathedral in the world. Many Ellington alumnae
> played or sang. Ella Fitzgerald sang *Solitude*, and that un-
> did me. This was true spiritual music, for me, and it set the
> bar for what we would do there in the future, although at
> that time I didn't even imagine having the chance to play
> there.
>
> — *Paul Winter*

Winter met The Very Reverend James Parks Morton, Dean
of New York's Cathedral of St. John the Divine, at a gathering of the Lindisfarne Association, a non-profit organization
founded by William Irwin Thompson to investigate the possibility of a new planetary culture. Morton was eager to engage the cathedral in issues bridging ecology and the arts;
and he found that his ambition and Winter's concerns and
activities were a good match. In 1980, Morton invited him to
be an artist-in-residence. Winter agreed. His comment was
that "it meant we could present almost any kind of event we
wanted there."

Making music at the Cathedral introduced Winter to
a new musical partner, the church's music director and organist, Paul Halley. His rich harmonic sense, sympathetic
ear, and orchestral imagination at the organ were well suited

to Winter's melodic sensibilities; and Halley's compositions and arrangements were created at the times of Winter's instrumental albums through 1998, among them the duets *Sun Singer* (1983, including percussionist Glen Velez on some tracks) and *Whales Alive* (1987).

As the first major project, Morton invited Paul Winter to develop a *Missa Gaia*, an *Earth Mass*, a liturgically-based celebration of the planet Earth. Winter was unfamiliar with the Catholic and Episcopal Mass, but after attending one at the Cathedral, he considered how he could construct a work organized on the major sections of the Mass — Kyrie, Sanctus, Agnus Dei, Gloria — for choir and the Consort. His idea emerged:

> I began imagining this Mass celebrating the Earth, using the different animal voices that have become part of our repertoire. I asked the dean, could we celebrate the entire Earth as a sacred space? Can we have the animal voices as celebrants in the Mass? Everything I asked him, he said was possible.

Jim Scott, who composed and arranged several portions of the work, explained to Paul Winter that the Mass is "like a concert with a symphony and since it's a musical form, we know about that..." What emerged was a work that encompassed Winter's favored Brazilian rhythms and the voices of animals. Winter and Scott traveled to the Cathedral several times to meet with choir director Paul Halley.

*Missa Gaia* took its form during and between rehearsals for a May 10, 1981 Mother's Day performance. The texts were drawn from a variety of sources, many of them innovative additions to the traditional Mass. The opening of *Missa Gaia* was Paul Winter's adaptation of a prayer by St. Francis of Assisi — *Canticle of Brother Sun* — sung by Susan Osborn and the choir:

> All praise be yours through Brother Sun, All praise be yours through Sister Moon, By Mother Earth my Lord be praised, By Brother Mountain, Sister Sea, Through Brother Wind and Brother Air, Through Sister Water, Brother Fire, The Stars above give thanks to thee, All praise to those who live in peace... Brother Sun, Sister Moon.

Jim Scott set the *Beatitudes* from the Gospel of St. Matthew 5: 3-12:

> Blessed are the poor in spirit, for theirs is the kingdom of heaven. Blessed are those who mourn, for they will be comforted. Blessed are the meek, for they will inherit the earth...

Scott's adaptation was alternately a contemplative canon and an upbeat anthem. Instrumental improvisations were interspersed throughout the work, providing contrasting moods. *For the Beauty of the Earth* was a Paul Winter saxophone solo, recorded in the Grand Canyon, with the sounds of the Colorado River as a backdrop. *Stained-Glass Morning* was a contemplative solo performed by Eugene Friesen. *Adoro Te Devote*, a Eucharistic hymn written by Thomas Aquinas, was accompanied by an Indian drone. *For the Beauty of the Earth*, a choral hymn followed. And Susan Osborn sang *Song of Praise*:

All of creation resounds with song, bless ye the Lord, praise Him forever... Stars in the heavens, waters below, bless ye the Lord, praise Him forever... Let all the the Earth, resound with joy, bless ye the Lord, praise Him forever...

This spirit of love of the planet was expressed in the contemporary hymn *The Blue Green Hills of Earth*, while the Mass movement *Agnus Dei* conveyed a spirit of yearning, synthesizing the Latin text with *Seal Eyes*. Winter's saxophone soared above the choir, followed by the haunting voices of seal pups.

Brazilian rhythms added a spirit of joyous celebration to the traditional Mass movements: *Kyrie* followed the pairing of Paul Winter's saxophone with the cry of a timber wolf, and *Sanctus* and *Benedictus* opened with the song of the humpback whale. Brazilian rhythms imbued percussionist Ted Moore's *Dance of Gaia* with rhythm, about which Paul Winter's program notes commented: "These drums speak of the power of the Earth... The interweave of lines among cello, oboe, sax and timpani elude to the symbiosis of energies that comprise the living *Gaia*."

A traditional Afro-Brazilian chant setting, *The Promise of a Fisherman*, enriched *Missa Gaia* with another aspect of that culture. *Missa Gaia* closed with an adaptation of St. Francis' *Canticle of Brother Sun*, framing the parting words, "Let Us Depart in Peace," with voices of the wolf, loon, and whale.

In her review of the recorded version of *Missa*

Gaia/*Earth Mass* (1982), Mary Kime captures the power and imagination of this work:

> It succeeds in providing through music an unmistakable intuition of the distance and magnitude of the universe, and of the unity of human life with animal life and with the cosmos itself. The sixteen sections of the *Missa Gaia* make use of musical idioms as varied as rhythmic drumming patterns of north-eastern Brazil, Gregorian chant, cantus firmus motet, polyphonic settings of melodic motifs taken from the cries of wolf, whale and loon, familiar hymns and contemporary jazz... Art here becomes not only imitation of nature but also a purposed way of expressing union with nature.

In addition to the *Missa Gaia*, and yet early in his artist residency, Paul Winter went further in his creativity to develop something huge and magnificent. He began to fashion a "happening" that would become an annual musical event. He referred to it as a *Solstice Celebration*:

> After receiving this open mandate from the Dean, I began thinking about what would be the most universal milestone we could celebrate at the cathedral, and it had occurred to me that it might be the winter solstice. So that December we presented what we called the Winter Consort Winter Solstice Whole Earth Christmas Celebration. The cathedral was filled, and the event was well-received, so we were encouraged to present a new version the following December. It then became an annual tradition. Over the years the winter solstice event evolved until it has become kind of an epic musical pageant with extensive staging, sound system, lighting and a giant sun-gong ris-

ing with its player 100 feet up into the vault of the cathedral... during the mid-90s, the production grew to include 20 dancers, 10 singers, and an expanded Consort...

There was also a *Summer Solstice,* a 4:30 am mid-June event, which was somewhat more modest. Paul Winter describes it as ...

> beginning in total darkness, with the light gradually joining the sounds, to usher in the dawning of the summer... when the sun is at its peak and the days abound with the promise of life's fullness. My dream, with this sunrise celebration, is to offer an experience of this resonance, in the mystical ambience of these early morning hours, through a deep listening journey within the awesome space of this largest cathedral in the world.

But *Winter Solstice* was not only grand in scale, it also attracted a large audience which eventually spread across three weekend performances. And early on it was adopted as an annual National Public Radio broadcast in New York City.

The structure of *Winter Solstice,* as it evolved through the 1980s and subsequently, dramatized the turning of the year in a climax that took place towards the latter part of the concert. The cathedral darkened, representing the longest night of the year. The near blackout was accompanied by dramatic jingling bells and small gongs suspended from a sculptural tree whose ornaments were struck by musicians and dancers. Light emerged out of darkness, the cathedral's inner walls became side-lit in glowing yellow as the sun returned, and a giant sun gong ascended the front end of the hall. After it peaked, a giant, blue and green Earth globe was lifted into the air, celebrating the vibrant life of the planet, evoking the image of the Earth as taken by astronauts aboard Apollo 8 as it orbited the moon.

Not being conventionally religious, Paul Winter had to find a way to mix his own Gaian spirituality with the Cathedral's Christianity, hence the original title of *Winter Solstice Whole Earth Christmas Celebration* situated *Winter Solstice* within a modestly Christian context.

Consort members during this early period included organist Paul Halley, percussionist Glen Valez, cellist Eugene Friesen, oboist Nancy Rumbel, and flutist Rhonda Larson. Among their recordings were *Wintersong* (1986) and the live recording *Spanish Angel* (1993). The Consort usually included a bassist (Russ Landau or Eliot Wadopian) and percussionist (Glen Velez or Jamey Haddad), and sometimes others, among them French horn player John Clark, and guitarist Oscar Castro-Neves. Having made periodic appearances with the Consort beginning in 1983, pianist Paul Sullivan eventually became a permanent member, following Halley's departure.

During the 1980s, *Winter Solstice* opened with a barrage of drums, introducing the lively *Tomorrow is My Dancing Day* followed by *Winter Song*. A solo by cellist Eugene Friesen, often showcased in Consort performances, provided a prelude to *Come Ye Worthy Gentlemen,* a work based on a traditional carol, performed on the piano by Paul Halley. The piece expanded into a rousing anthemic song with a driving rhythm. Winter then welcomed the crowd, introducing gospel singer Kecia Lewis-Evans, who had just joined the ensemble to sing a virtuoso rendition of *His Eye Is On The Sparrow*, an inspirational religious song popular in the Black church. The song, in later years sung by Theresa Thomason, became a regular part of the Winter Solstice concert repertoire. After an enthusiastic audience response, the gospel hymn was briefly reprised, and Winter next took the microphone to introduce a shift in tone:

> I don't know anything on land that can follow that, so we're going to jump into the ocean and bring you with us if you will. Just for fun I'd like to imagine we were invited to a party under the sea and whales from oceans all over the world came to sing with us. We have humpback whales from Hawaii and Bermuda, and Puerto Rico, and other places and we've put them together as a cetacean party here. And we're going to make some new music with them and see where they might take us in this journey into the sea from *Whales Alive*.

What followed was a rich collage of whale songs. After about two minutes, Winter's soprano saxophone entered the mix, introducing melodic elements that responded to the whale calls, which eventually faded. Winter continued solo, moving into more sustained melody, which was joined by the Cathedral's organist. The piece concluded with the famous humpback whale songs recorded in the late 1960s, first used to open his *Lullaby for the Great Mother Whale for the Sea Pups*.

Flutist Rhonda Larson shifted the mood with an ornate solo piece, leading to a collaboration with a pre-recorded performance by the Dmitri Pokrovsky Singers of a lively, rhythmic village song titled *Kurski Funk*. In future concerts around the world that included elements of *Winter Solstice*, the Singers joined Winter in person. They appeared on the album *Earth Beat* (1987), recorded in Moscow.

At this point, the musical-ritual *Winter Solstice* enactment began in the darkened Cathedral with *The Turning Point Suite*. The opening section was an improvisation featuring sustained tones and brief melodic gestures by the melody instruments. It was followed by low rumbling percussion, sparse at first, then building to a climax with crashing cymbals and organ clusters, then fading, replaced, at first light, by ringing bells and blaring brass sounds. Sustained pipe organ textures then filled the space as the sun appeared while the music assumed the form of a dramatic organ prelude, increasingly mysterious, then calmer towards its conclusion.

Out of the silence, Paul Winter's saxophone intoned a simple statement of the lyrical ballad *Sun Singer*. In a subsequent interview, Winter stated:

> I'd like to invite people to come with a sense of adventure, to have perhaps some new musical experience and also to go deeper into themselves. I want to take people on a journey, and bring them home.

The drama was followed by Paul Halley's optimistic hymn, *Sound Over All the Water*, sung by Kecia Lewis-Evans. The song had been originally one of Susan Osborn's featured pieces a decade earlier with the Consort. It was also included on Susan Osborn's 1982 album titled *Signature*. It continued to be a hallmark of Winter's Solstice concerts, and it became an item in the repertoire of school and church choirs around the United States.

Panpipes initiated another hymn, *The Song For the World*, also with the Pokrovsky Singers, and dedicated "to the homeless." It was followed by a spikey rhythmic tune, and then a cello-piano duet by Eugene Friesen and Paul Halley. At that point, Winter spoke of an early conversation with folksinger Pete Seeger. The two had met at the 1966 Newport Folk Festival where Winter was invited to perform as an Amadinda (Ugandan log marimba) player. Seeger had mused about the possibility of creating a new synthesis, "something of the essence of classical music and combine it with some of the essences of folk music and ethnic music, in which I included jazz, from around the world, and see if some new music could be woven from that."

Winter recalled Seeger pointing out that "the key thing is participation... to involve people with making music with you," something that Winter noted as" the guiding word for the Consort." With that, Pete Seeger came on stage to sing, with the audience joining in, *My Rainbow Race*. The refrain is: "One blue sky above us, one ocean lapping all our shore / One earth so green and round, who could ask for more? / And because I love you I'll give it one more try / To show my rainbow race, it's too soon to die."

Kecia Lewis-Evans returned to the stage to sing a

Christmas hymn "Christ was born in Bethlehem / Hallelujah…" to the melody of the spiritual "Michael Row Your Boat Ashore." She began *a cappella*, soon joined by the Cathedral organ, and closed with Paul Winter's broad saxophone solo over the vocals. An early Consort favorite *Minuit* transitioned into the carol *Oh Come All Ye Faithful*, dramatically closing out the concert.

In subsequent years, the *Winter Solstice* dramatization took on a more formalized structure. The evolving conception of the concerts, as documented on the recording *Silver Solstice* (2005), assumed the title *Journey Through the Longest Night*. Its core sections were titled *Solstice Tree*, *Storm*, *Bells of Solstice*, and *Return of the Sun*. Each event maximized the use of space within the world's largest cathedral, St. John the Divine, in New York City. This narrative arc helped give the performances an overarching shape.

The sense of drama continued to be heightened by elaborate lightening, sculptural props, stage choreography, use of the entirety of the Cathedral from floor to ceiling and end to end to situate musical and other events, and the presence of special guest singers and dance ensembles. Guest performers represented a tremendous diversity of cultures around the globe. Most years, a core tradition of the Winter Solstice experience was an audience participation collective human *howl 'e'lujah* chorus, following a performance of *Wolf Eyes*, a composition that incorporated recorded wolf calls.

For many, a highlight of Winter Solstice, beginning

in the 1994, was the appearance of a new featured vocal soloist, gospel singer Teresa Thomason. In 2023, Paul Winter referred to Thomason as "the 'star 'of our solstice celebrations for over 25 years." In a 2021 interview, Thomason reflected upon her first experiences in this setting:

> First time singing at Solstice is truly an experience. You can't call it a concert. You had to practice coming in and out, and off this humongous stage with the audience on both sides of you, front and back. You were there, spinning and trying to communicate with both sides of the audience. There was lights and cameras and the beautiful ambience of the Cathedral.

*Theresa Thomason, performing with the Consort in Worcester, 2024*

For Theresa Thomason, the Cathedral of St. John the Divine has been a special space in which to sing:

> You have the right to be as soulful and down home as you want. The Cathedral to me touches all of your senses as you sing. The sound is so big and surrounds you. It feels more like a physical experience.

Thomason brought a long career as a singer of gospel and Rhythm and Blues. She first gained attention in the Black Church when she was thirteen years old, and she won Amateur Night at the Apollo Theater. Thomason gained radio play with an R&B hit dance song, "Fresh Enuff." She built a career touring with The Inspirations and with other gospel groups. Her musical interests have always been expansive, as she recalls: "I grew up listening to everything from rock to R&B to World Music to classical. I found relevance in all of them."

Her solo career has included appearances with Stevie Wonder, Ray Charles, Pete Seeger, and Valerie Simpson. The music-beyond-category nature of the Paul Winter Consort has strongly appealed to Thomason, and for decades she has brought her very distinct musical personality and presence to the lineage of Consort vocalists.

In the 2010s, the twenty-five dancers and drummers of the Forces of Nature Dance Theatre Company became an annual feature of Winter Solstice. The Company, founded in 1981 and led by artistic director and choreographer Abdel Salaam, is devoted to transmitting "positive values, traditions and beliefs of the people and cultures of the Americas, Africa and the African Diaspora." The Company's integration of dance and ritual, bright costumes and joyful performance within set pieces interspersed throughout the Solstice event, deepened the overall experience of Winter Solstice.

The spectacular events presented by Paul Winter sought to address something of an earthly, if not celestial proportion:

> Observing this key moment in the relationship of the Earth to our Sun gives us a rare opportunity to get in touch with the fact that we live in and are part of a solar system, which itself is a particle of our galaxy, the Milky Way, which in turn is one of billions of galaxies in the great universe.

The goals of Paul Winter's *Solstice* events align with the overarching aims of his career: to explore, simultaneously, the inner life of people, the human connection to animals and the environment, and the place of all species within the vast cosmos. *Solstice* was emblematic of the expansion of his interests and vision first explored with the early Consorts and later with the Connecticut *Town Meeting* of 1974. Winter's work continues to model a path beyond human myopia to celebrate the creative and ethical potential of humankind and the depth and breadth of the expressive voices of all species.

[following page:] *Enrique Eisenmann, Theresa Thomason, Peter Slavov, Paul Winter, Rogério Boccato  and Eugene Friesen, performing in the Winter Consort, Worcester, Dec. 2024*

## 14. Epilogue

Paul Winter's creative output is now in its seventh decade. In recent years he has continued his annual events that mark the cycles of Earth's seasons, and continued to compose and perform new music that broaden his repertoire. Paul Winter's remarkable run continues.

Winter's devotion to environmental concerns never ceases to find new creative outlets. He was among the thirty-six artists, serving as resident sax player through the ten-day, 2017 "Bringing the Dead Sea to Life Through Art and Music" symposium in Israel and Jordan. Its goal was build awareness of climate risks impacting the Dead Sea. The event opened with a concert by the Consort, the premiere of "Music of Birds," from Winter's unfolding "Flyways" project. This is "a celebration of the great bird migration from southern Africa up the Rift Valley through the Middle East to Eurasia, and back."

Winter brought on tour a series of "This Glorious Earth" concerts in Spring 2023. These duet performances joined Winter with pianist Henrique Eisenmann and the recorded sounds of wolves, whales and a wood thrush living on Winter's farm in Northwest Connecticut. Winter interwove personal narrative about his musical experiences within the natural world. Paul Winter's collaboration with Enrique Eisenmann, a young Brazilian pianist and faculty member at the New England Conservatory, began around the Covid-19 pandemic lockdowns. Eisenmann has become Paul Winter's most constant musical collaborator.

Like many musicians during the pandemic, Paul Winter re-centered his productions in an adaptive manner. For Winter, his home base in his Connecticut barn became his core performance space for internet streamed performances, supplemented by video releases. Rather than cancel the scheduled June 2020 Summer Solstice event, Winter live streamed a concert melding a small group of performers in his barn with remotely recorded performances by additional musicians.

The 2021 Summer Solstice Celebration reunited Winter with singer Theresa Thomason and cellist Eugene Friesen, adding Eisenmann and bassoonist Jeff Boratko. A recording of the performance was released the next year as *Concert From the Barn.* Following one further live streamed Summer Solstice event, in 2022, The Cathedral of St. John the Divine in New York City once again became its home in 2023.

Mounting the Winter Solstice Celebration during the pandemic, for forty years a fixture at the Cathedral of St. John the Divine, presented a greater challenge. In place of the December 2020 and 2021 live events, video compilations were made available. The 2020 video, "Everybody Under the Sun," featured performances spanning four decades of previous shows. In 2022, a second video release stood in for the live Cathedral event. "Winter Solstice: The Early Years" represented the complete performance in 1988. Ironically, and fortunate for readers, this is the concert I detailed in the first edition of this book. Another retrospective Winter Solstice Celebration video, *Solstice Saga*, was released in 2023 on YouTube.

As he sought to address the pandemic era as an opportunity, Paul Winter crafted a Spring 2020 series of educational "Sonic Saturdays" videos, released on YouTube. Topics included the music of songbirds and the "benefits of listening to music to help your memory and focus."

The Winter Solstice Celebration assumed a new touring format beginning in 2023. Paul Winter had returned to public performance in 2022, initially by playing solo and in duet with Enrique Eisenmann.

The next Winter Solstice events before a live audience required serious rethinking. Returning to the Cathedral of St. John the Divine proved not to be possible. Winter reassembled the small group that had performed the live-streamed Autumn Equinox show from Winter's barn in September 2020. They presented the musical side of the Solstice repertoire without dancers or other theatrical elements. This Consort featured Paul Winter veterans vocalist Theresa Thomason and cellist Eugene Friesen, with Winter, Enrique Eisenmann, bassist Peter Slavov, and drummer Rogério Boccato. The 2023 Winter Solstice tour made four stops in New England and Troy, New York. In 2024, the tour grew to encompass ten sites in the same region.

The influence on Paul Winter of the composer Charles Ives was highlighted in the eighth chapter of this book, "Musical Spectacle." To recap, in the mid-1970s, Winter organized several concerts to mark the Centennial of Ives' birth. These began with the August 1974 "Musical Town Meeting" at the Ives homestead in Danbury, Connecticut.

Nearly 50 years later, Winter returned to the theme of Ives, revisiting in a quartet format, Ives' concept of a "Universe Symphony." Ives' original work for multiple orchestras was left incomplete during his lifetime. Several reconstructions were performed in the 1990s. The structure was organized around three thematic movements, addressing past, present, and future. Winter's August 2023 concert, at Yale University, was titled "Adventures in the Universe." Winter articulated his conception of the evening in this way:

> Our aspiration is to use the extraordinary acoustics of Woolsey Hall to create soundscapes which might awaken in the imaginations of listeners, and players, some inkling of a perspective of the vastness of the Universe, and, as well, to remind us of the uniqueness and preciousness of our planetary home, the Earth.

"Adventures in the Universe" is an apt point on which to close a discussion of Paul Winter's "Musical World." It exemplifies Winter's unceasing desire to explore new ideas, places, musicians, and species to sonically convey the grandeur of this planet and its inhabitants. He has never ceased to maintain the seasonal and other traditions he has established over many years. Paul Winter's fascination balancing the new and the old, and the human with other species continues to energize his multi-faceted musical career.

## Notes and Sources

The first edition of *Music World of Paul* Winter was released as an eBook by Intelligent Arts in March 2019, my first book to be written with a general audience in mind. Hence the narrative focus of its text and lack of sourcing and end notes in that edition. For information about how to access this book in eBook formats, see: https://intelligentarts.net/paulwinter/

While many articles about Paul Winter have appeared in the press over the years, most focus on specific events. I have drawn upon my personal collection of documentation from Winter's concerts dating back to the 1970s. Winter has only periodically given extensive interviews, the most significant of which are those conducted and published by Michael Bourne, Duncan Heining, Meagan Meehan, Patty Lee Parmalee, David Rothenberg, and Tony Vellela. I found, while working on the book, that these sources offered a comprehensive public record of Winter's statements to date regarding his musical development, family history, musical evolution, and life mission. Winter's own web and social media presence had provided additional materials. All quotations in my book draw upon the public record and their sources are listed in the after notes and bibliography.

All quotations from David Darling, Susan Osborn, and Jim Scott are from interviews I personally conducted. Writing this book naturally involved extensive research beyond the firsthand accounts contained in these interviews. In addition to searching the public record and published accounts, research included substantial close musical listening and reflections upon my own personal experience of Paul Winter's musical career. This was a truly rewarding project. I emerged with even greater admiration for the work of Paul Winter, particularly in the context of these difficult times.

## Preface

*use of the term "song" from bird song research applied to whales*

"Spectrographic analysis shows, however, that all prolonged vocalizations occur in long, fixed sequences and are repe*ated with considerable accuracy* every few minutes. Because one of the characteristics of bird songs is that they are fixed patterns of sounds that are repeated, we call the fixed patterns of humpback sounds "songs." The principal differences between bird and humpback songs are that bird songs usually last for a few seconds, while humpback songs last for minutes; and one song of a bird is usually separated from the next by a period of silence. whereas humpback songs are repeated without a significant pause or break in the rhythm of singing." Payne and McVay 1971, 590.

## Chapter 2.An aspiring young jazz musician

*Winter developed a reputation as a soloist*

Soon after taking up the clarinet, Winter and his sister Diane, a pianist who later became a Suzuki piano teacher, began to perform publicly as a duo. A fall 1949 performance was reported in the local newspaper. The *Rhapsody in Blue* performance as a pianist was preceded by an appearance as clarinet soloist (in "Dizzy Fingers") in seventh grade; each of these with the high school band.

*access to the music and to this community of musicians*

Winter adds: "I had the advantage of having a whole city to draw from; and it was a great jazz city, then. Lots of bebop happening; the South Side of Chicago was just roaring with bebop. I spent most of my nights driving from Evanston on the North Side of Chicago down to the South Side, hanging out in jazz clubs. I was just enthralled with that music. And we just had a super little band."

*pianist Warren Bernhardt, bassist Richard Evans, and drummer Harold Jones*

Evans was an early member of the Sun Ra Arkestra, and then a studio arranger/producer, and professor at the Berklee College of Music; Jones was most notably a five-year member of the Basie band, and band member backing Sarah Vaughn and others. The Sextet was Bernhardt's first recording credit; subsequently he recorded with folk and jazz musicians (Tom Rush, Tim Hardin, Richie Havens, Carly Simon...) and as a band leader.

*arrangements were purchased from Jimmy Heath*

Others were written by band members bassist Richard Evans and pianist Warren Bernhardt; Winter himself did arrangements for their recordings *Jazz Meets the Bossa Nova* and *Jazz Meets the Folk Song*). Winter also loved saxophonist Stan Getz's *Focus*: "with strings... you don't know in those pieces where the improvising begins and the writing stops, you don't know which is which. That's my standard."

*In 1961, the band won first place*

This victory, in May of his senior year, came as a surprise, although the band's placed second in the Notre Dame Collegiate Jazz Festival, a month prior.

## Chapter 4.          A New Consort: *Road*, and *Icarus*

*guitarist/pianist Ralph Towner*

In an interview with Mario Calvitti, Towner recalled: "... my mother was a piano teacher but I was such a stubborn child and I refused to take lessons from her, I would just listen to all the piano lessons in the back of the room. I always had this particular gift; composing and improvising is something I did naturally from the very beginning." He learned jazz standards on trumpet, accompanied by his mother; he learned the music by ear from his brother's big band and from Nat King Cole Trio records. He told Anil Prasad: "I played trumpet in Dixieland, polka and swing bands from the time I was seven or eight years old. I would improvise in my little school band during the concerts. It was always during the school songs and marches. So, I could always improvise. That was my strong suit as far as jazz time feeling. It's a tricky thing to get. You really have to play your way into it, I think." Towner continues to describe himself as "a piano player who plays guitar. It's always been my approach to the instrument." Again, from the Calvitti interview: "[My] improvisational style] comes from being a pianist. My intention was to use guitar as a piano and with the same approach, including being able to play each note in a chord, control the volume of every note (like bring one note out and let the others perfectly even). This is a piano technique, classical, when you play an accompaniment for yourself and you have the main line you don't play the accompaniment so loud that you can't hear the theme."

*David Darling*

Jim Scott, a member of a subsequent incarnation of the Consort said: "When David Darling plays, the music's going along and he plays just one note. That's not necessarily 'David the virtuoso'; it's that the music was going along one way and then 'the cello comes in!' And he makes that life-changing."

*even though we began playing Ralph's music*

Darling adds: "Ralph wanted us to play more of his music, but there was some resistance from Paul from time to time."

*Winter invited producer George Martin ... to oversee the album*

Chris Michie: "The interesting thing about the Paul Winter album was that, when it came back to AIR London for mixing, there were multitracks of the songs from two sets of sessions, done at different times in different studios, edited together, basically bar by bar. They had totally different sounds, so the bass sound would change from one cut to the next. It was mixed edit by edit: they'd set up a mix and mix that section, and then, of course, the tape would run on into the next section, at which point the mix would totally go to hell. Then they'd set up for that next section and try to match the one before and so on, then edit the 2-track tape together at the same point as the multitrack edit. It was a very painstaking process."

## Chapter 6.        Electric Winter

*David Darling continued to perform with Winter until 1982*

Darling relates: "I grew up into life touring with the Consort and raising a family, at the same time. In the very beginning my family traveled with us. When we just had one baby we were on the road together. One, Jessica, when she was four, she was ready to go to preschool. That's when we settled into a place in Bethel, Connecticut; she went to preschool there. They said at school, they would say, 'Jessica won't talk to the other kids, she only wants to talk to us adults.' Jessica, of course, grew up talking to adults all the time."

## Chapter 7.    Consort Anew

*"I mimicked the gestures*

*Munroe Review,"* For Grammy Winner Eugene Friesen, a special Fresno Pacific concert means coming home," March 18, 2023. https://munroreview.com/2023/03/18/for-grammy-winner-eugene-friesen-a-special-fresno-pacific-concert-means-coming-home/, accessed January 2, 2025.

*spontaneous improvisation*

Bob Protzman, "Cellist Friesen Takes Music Into A New Age," The Chicago Tribune (Knight-Ridder Newspapers syndicated column), December 11, 1986, 60.

*give birth to what Jung called... Sometimes I'll sit down to practice one thing:*

Natasha Jaffee, "An Interview with Eugene Friesen: Cellist, Improviser, Composer, and Educator." https://natashajaffe.com/home. Accessed January 2, 2025.

*Afrological stream of music*

Jaffee interview.

## Chapter 8.        Winter and Wolves

*Bernie Krause invented the term "biophony"*

Krause engages in recordings of natural environments around the world; earlier in his career, in 1964, Krause and Paul Beaver worked with the early Moog synthesizer; their work includes *The Nonesuch Guide to Electronic Music* (1967).

*This was not a domesticated animal by any means*

Susan Osborn: "This wolf's name was Slick and was born in captivity, so it was never really suited to live in the wild. But it still smelled wild. You could smell, you know, a scent of wild animals. And this was a wild animal and just barely on the side of civilized. I didn't really ever feel like I was in danger in any way. It was just that this animal was smarter than me in a lot of ways. We had the opportunity to tour with Slick during one season. The thing about this particular wolf is that he didn't like men, and he really liked women. He would go to women. I always felt that it was scent; there's some biochemical thing going on, a difference between men and women that the wolf sensed. I didn't feel like this was a dog in anyway. This was not; the only thing tame about this animal is that it was willing to be on a chain, and would come, you know, would follow his handler. But this was another thing."

## Chapter 10.                    Communing with Whales

*"Celebration of the Whale"*

California governor Edmund "Jerry" Brown Jr. hosted the "Celebration of the Whale" on November 20, 1976. Several-thousand people attended what Brown referred to as "[an] opportunity for people to enjoy themselves, to learn, to celebrate" whales. The Governor expressed the hope that "as a mammal, their survival is symbolic of our own." While the fair, comprised of "exhibits of environmental groups, state agencies and private firms," was reportedly funded by big businesses, an evening concert at the Sacramento Memorial Auditorium "was the real money raiser. Those fortunate enough to obtain a $4.00 ticket were treated to six hours of entertainment which included a beautiful color documentary of whales narrated in person by researcher Dr. Roger Payne. In addition, there was the kick-ass music of Country Joe McDonald, the spirited Paul Winter Consort, John Sebastian, the lamentable Fred Neil, and the headliner, Joni Mitchell."

*For want of a better concept we call it intelligence*

For another, non-musical, example of sea mammal intelligence, consider Dudzinski and Frohoff's observation: "dolphins can recognize themselves in mirrors; only humans, some of the great apes, and elephants have been demonstrated to show this ability with dolphins. In other words, although humans and dolphins lack a common ancestor, they have evolved similar cognitive abilities, possibly for comparable social or communicative *reasons*." Joan McIntyre points out that "what we test and recognize is limited by the questions we can devise and our ability to conceive of a system in which those questions are meaningful."

*human music could build upon adapted whale motifs*

There are numerous examples of human musical compositions, in addition to those of Paul Winter. Here is a brief description of two of the best known examples, each dating to the early 1970s. Descriptions of Winter's music based upon whale motifs appears in Chapter 11.

Alan Hovhaness' symphonic poem *And God Created Great Whales*, Op. 229, No. 1 (1970) combines unison pentatonic melodies, quartal harmonies, and at 2:40, humpback whale recordings by the Paynes (soon to appear on *Songs of the Humpback Whales*), joined by rapid melodic figures in the strings. A string and percussion crescendo leads to a grand unison melody in the brass section. At 4:20, there is a brief passage of downward horn glissandi, imitative of whale motifs, followed by a return of the busy string activity. This segues into a full minute of unaccompanied recorded whale song. A brief interlude of orchestral bells and harp provides a transition (at 7:05) to delicate flute and string interplay, and then solo violin glissandi, calling and responding. The whale sounds return at 7:50, soon joined (until 9:45) by quiet, textural violin interplay. A closing pentatonic melody in the strings (10:05), punctuated by sharp sustained tone brass clusters, and (at 10:35), a series of long crescendo alternating with textural passages, presaging (at 10:25) low pitched recorded whale motifs, increasingly joined by busy string and then brass figures. A crescendo of percussion provides a dramatic closing.

George Crumb composed *Vox Balaenae* ("Voice of the Whale), for Three Masked Players (amplified flute, cello, and piano) in 1971. Black eye masks garb the human presence. Like many of Crumb's works (I have performed several, including *Vox Balaenae*), the composer makes broad use of extended instrumental techniques, among them singing into the flute, strumming and plucking the piano strings, holding down and sliding a finger over the piano strings while playing a note, the use of harmonics on all three instruments, lip whistles. The music is more suggestive than imitative of whale motifs. Pizzicato cello notes slide from one to the next over a ringing drone made by a scraped piano string in the lower register. Ringing, percussive strikes of the piano strings suggest the depths of the sea. Echoing cello harmonics, played simultaneously with descending glissandi suggest sea gulls. The music encompasses a broad range of pitches, suggesting the frequency span of whale song. Overall, this sparse, often quiet work sets an otherworldly mood, maybe one of the depths of the sea.

## Chapter 11.                    Celebrating the Music of Whales

*As the composition begins*

This writer, a fan of the grainy, at moments broken, timbre of late-period John Coltrane's tenor saxophone wondered about how similar is the second whale sound (the response) and that of Coltrane.

*Rare among Winter's music, it features a vocal*

Other examples include, from the early period of the Consort, *Minuit* and *The Silence of a Candle*; from *Common Ground*, the title track and "Ancient Voices"; from the late 1970s, the songs associated with Susan Osborn and Jim Scott, among them vocal segments of *Missa Gaia*; collaborations with the Dimitri Prokofsky Singers and with Pete Seeger; and most recently, songs with gospel singer Theresa Thomason.

*"I'm a musician, not a naturalist"*

Winter commented in an interview: "...It's so much more intriguing for journalists to talk about wolves and whales or going to Russia, but these are just things we're enthused about that happen to be reflected in the music. Most pop music is based on people's enthusiasm for their lovers. It's really no different to be enthused about the Grand Canyon. What I'm most interested in is the music itself."

## Chapter 12.     Musical Spectacle

*the "Noss Jollity Company" vaudeville troupe*

*The Times* (Philadelphia) announced the vaudeville troupe's Philadelphia performance: "A bright and sparkling entertainment is announced for the Standard Theatre this week, when the Noss Jollity Company will present for the first time in this city their fantastic musical comedy, 'The Kodak [in Three Snap Shots]' as the title indicates, the play is a series of snap-shots at all sorts of people; queer, quaint and curious. The plot, though not featured, is more distinct than is usually found in a farce comedy, and tells a story that *will* appeal to all.... [It is a] new fantastic musical comedy... as bright as a dollar fresh from the mint...."

*the population of Altoona reached 40,000*

Located in south central Pennsylvania, Altoona was, from its inception, a railroad town. Pennsylvania Railroad founded the town in 1849 to house its main train construction and repair facilities. Steam engine trains moved coal, consumer goods, and as the Civil War began, Union troops and munitions. At the time, the railroads and canals, such as the Erie Canal in New York State, vied for dominance as a form of transportation. The town was strategically located near Allegheny Mountain foothills, en route to the expanding American west. The construction of the nearby half-mile-long Horseshoe Curve, in 1854, allowed trains to safely traverse the mountain slopes connecting Eastern and Western Pennsylvania, giving railroads an edge. As train tracks were being laid at a rapidly expanding rate in Pennsylvania, train construction steadily boomed, and with it, Altoona.

The Winter family was civic minded; Paul Sr. joined the Altoona Rotary Club a year after his marriage to Beulah Harnish, and remained a member for the latter 51 years of his century-long life. Arthur was a charter member and served as its 11th president in the late 1920s, and as its district governor in the early 1930s. Many years later, in 2003, their store was recognized as a "Heritage Honoree" of the Blair County Business Hall of Fame honoring companies in business for more than 25 years and showing "a lasting impact on commerce generated from Blair County." Paul Sr. and his wife, Beulah (Harnish) were involved in their son's school's music program.

*Winter assembled a 17-member Consort to celebrate Ives '100th anniversary*

A year after this 1974 "Musical Town Meeting," Winter brought a second edition, "Para-Desa," to the Mathews farm. The Ives homestead performance was repeated subsequently at Yale University, at a 1976 American Bicentennial at Kennedy Center in Washington, D.C, and taken on tour.

For the third of the Consort's engagements with the Indianapolis Symphony (a previous collaboration was the final performance of the second Consort), Jim Scott did the arrangements on short notice and limited budget, drawing upon music from *Common Ground* and *Callings*. Members of the Consort furiously copied parts at the last minute. Scott recalls young conductor Paul Polivnik giving the orchestra an impassioned speech to rally their spirited engagement; at the time, convincing orchestras to engage with new music could be challenging. In this case, the perceived difficulty was no doubt heightened by the inclusion of recorded sounds from wolves and sea mammals. The concert was ultimately received well by both the audience and by members of the orchestra.

## Chapter 13.                    Solstice

*the Lindisfarne Association*

The Schumacher Center for New Economics website, which hosts transcripts of talks given at the Lindisfarne Association, offers this historical background: "In 1972 William Irwin Thompson founded the Lindisfarne Association as an alternative way for the humanities to develop in a scientific and technical civilization. Lindisfarne became an association of scientists, artists, scholars, and contemplatives devoted to the study and realization of a new planetary culture. Lindisfarne began its activities in Southampton, New York, in 1973, then moved to Manhattan in 1976, and finally in 1979 to Crestone, Colorado, where today the Lindisfarne Fellows House, the Lindisfarne Chapel, and the Lindisfarne Mountain Retreat are under the ownership and management of the Crestone Mountain Zen Center. In 1997 Thompson retired from the presidency of the Lindisfarne Association; in 2009 the Association disbanded as a formal not-for-profit organization. The Lindisfarne Fellows, however, voted to continue their fellowship as an informal association of creative individuals interested in one another's work..."

*Canticle of Brother Sun*

Scott included within this movement "the Canticle... an instrumental riff that we played with the Indianapolis Symphony. Paul said, 'what if we use that in there as the melody; can we use that?' So that ended up being in there."

*Later during the 1980s, Winter Solstice opened with*

This particular example is from a December 17, 1988 radio broadcast.

*Winter spoke of an early conversation with folksinger Pete Seeger*

Paul Winter had become interested in folk music while touring Latin America in the 1960s. He was impressed by Seeger's music when he sat, at John Hammond's invitation, in the recording booth for Seeger's 1964 Carnegie Hall concert. Winter was invited by a friend of Peter Yarrow, Andrew Tracey, to join him as one of three Amadinda (Ugandan log marimba) players at the 1966 Newport Folk Festival. There, he met Pete Seeger. They became long, term friends and, in 1996, recorded and produced the record Pete in Winter's barn.

*as documented on the recording Silver Solstice (2005)*

Previous Solstice concerts were released on the recordings *Solstice Live* (1993), *Celtic Solstice* (1999), *Solstice Gems* (2002).

*the 'star' of our solstice celebrations*

Paul Winter's press announcement of the 2023 Winter Solstice tour of New England venues that replaced the the event at the Cathedral of St. John the Divine.

*First time singing at Solstice*

Video interview of Theresa Thomason posted on Paul Winter's Facebook page, December 8, 2021.

*Apollo Theater..., hit dance song, "Fresh Enuff"... The Inspirations*

Program notes to "A Pretty Good Concert" with Chorus Angelicus and Gaudeamus and The Paul Winter Consort, Music Shed on the Ellen Battell Stoeckel Estate, Norfolk, Connecticut, June 15-16, 1996.

*I grew up listening to... You have the right... I grew up listening... Her solo career has included...*

Mike Horyczun, *Theresa Thomason adds show-stopping vocals to Solstice celebrations, The Hour*, Dec 8, 2017.

https://www.thehour.com/news/article/Theresa-Thomason-adds-show-stopping-vocals-to-12415934.php. Accessed January 3, 2025.

*positive values, traditions and beliefs*

Forces of Nature Dance Theater company website: https://www.forcesofnature.org/programs

*Observing this key moment*

"Paul Winter's Solstice Celebrations: Summer." Paul Winter website but no longer accessible. http://solsticeconcert.com/summersolstice/#venue. Accessed May 17, 2018.

**Chapter 14.**            **Epilogue**

*a celebration of the great bird migration*

Quotation from Paul Winter's "Earth Music" webpage, at https://paulwinter.com/mfe/. Accessed December 5, 2024.

*The 2021 Summer Solstice Celebration reunited Winter with singer Theresa Thomason*

This marked their Summer Solstice reunion, while not their first Covid-era performance together. This had taken place at the live streamed September 2020 Autumn Equinox Celebration in Winter's barn.

Information about Paul Winter's pandemic era projects and performances was collected from the events calendar on his webpage, Facebook postings, and reports by numerous media outlets.

**Bibliography**

Altoona High School Alumni Directory, 1921, Part 1, 1877-1909, Blair County, PA; http://files.usgwarchives.net/pa/blair/education/ahsalumn1-1.txt. Accessed June 5, 2018.

*Altoona Mirror*, October 8, 1956, 3. Newspaper Archives: https://newspaperarchive.com/altoona-mirror-oct-08-1956-p-3. Accessed June 5, 2018.

*Altoona Tribune*, "Theodore Roosevelt Junior High School Parents ' Music Club," October 5, 1949, 2.

"Altoona," Wikipedia. https://en.m.wikipedia.org/wiki/Altoona,_Pennsylvania. Accessed June 5, 2018.

"I Love Altoona" website. http://www.ilovealtoona.com/history/. Accessed June 5, 2018.

American Rails website, http://www.american-rails.com/states.html; http://www.american-rails.com/pa.html. Accessed June 5, 2018.

Artist Direct website, "Paul Winter," http://www.artistdirect.com/artist/bio/paul-winter/510924. Accessed July 23, 2017.

Battersby Duo, "For the Love of Pete." *Huffington Post* (blog), June 16, 2016 (updated June 17, 2017). http://www.huffingtonpost.com/battersby-duo/for-the-love-of-pete_b_9789952.html. Accessed June 5, 2018.

Anne Beecher, "Paul Winter," *American environmental leaders: from Colonial times to the present.*" Vol. 2, 2000, 866-868.

Thomas Berry, *The Dream of the Earth*. Berkeley: Counterpoint Press, (1988), 2015.

Thomas Berry, "The Wild and the Sacred," *The Great Work: Our Way into the Future*, New York: Harmony/Bell Tower, 1999.

John R. Beyer, President's Report, "No 'Historic 'First Woman in the Rotary Club of Altoona." 4th History of the Rotary Club of Altoona, 1987, and 41, 53, http://www.rotaryofaltoona.org/2013%204th%20HISTORY%20of%20the%20ROTARY%20CLUB%20of%20Altoona.pdf. Accessed June 5, 2018.

John Beyer PP and Dick Fruth PP, "Rotarians in the Blair County Business Hall of Fame." February 2013, 152-153.

Tim Blangger, "Paul Winter's Nature is to Change Musical Environments." *The Morning* Call (Allentown, PA), September 1, 2000.

Michael Bourne, Paul Winter: One World Music, *Down Beat*, May 1986, 26-28, 56.

Terry Breen, "A Winter's Tale: Paul Winter takes inspiration from the earth and its creatures to make music that is out of this world." *Northwestern*, Spring 2000.

Mario Calvitti, Interview with Ralph Towner, *All About Jazz*. May 16, 2017, https://www.allaboutjazz.com/ralph-towner-the-accidental-guitarist-ralph-towner-by-mario-calvitti.php?page=1. Accessed June 5, 2018.

*Canyon Consort: The Paul Winter Consort in the Grand Canyon* (VHS video). David Vassar, director, A&M, 1985.

Ludwig N. Carbyn, "Wolf Howling as a Technique to Ecosystem Interpretation in National Parks," The Behavior and Ecology of Wolves. *Proceedings of the Symposium on the Behavior and Ecology of Wolves, 1975.*" New York: Garland STPM Press, 1979, 458-470.

Lynn Hunter Cline, "Paul Winter: Making Music for Planet Earth." *Body Mind Spirit* 14:3, May 1995.

David Darling, "Improvisation Class, Omega Institute, Summary," unpublished workshop handout, Summer 1987.

Dayton Daily News, "Paul Winter Consort Naturally in Tune No Matter the Season." September 20, 1991, 25.

*Delaware County Daily Times* (Upper Darby, PA), August 2, 1994.

Bill Devall, *Simple in Means, Rich in Ends: Practicing Deep Ecology.* Salt Lake City: Peregrine Smith Books, 1988.

John Dilberto, "Oregon: Beauty, and the Beat." Down Beat, February 1988, 25 of 24-26.

Donna Doherty, "Paul Winter Consort helps ONE celebrate its 35th anniversary and honor Earth." *New Haven* Register (CT), April 19, 2009.

Kathleen M. Dudzinski and Toni Frohoff, *Dolphin Mysteries: Unlocking the Secrets of Communication.* New Haven: Yale University Press, 2008.

*Echoes.* "Paul Winter at 70: An Icon of Global Fusion: Paul Winter turned 70 last Monday, on August 31." https://echoes.org/2009/09/06/paul-winter-at-70/https://echoes.org/2009/09/06/paul-winter-at-70/. Accessed June 5, 2018.

Bradley P. Ethington, "Charles Ives's 'Country Band 'March: Its Appearance in Three of His Major Works." *WASBE Journal* (World Association for Symphonic Bands and Ensembles) 10, 2003, 106-110.

Janis Gibson, "Winter recalls his time here." *The Redding Pilot* (CT), September 9, 2010, 2A.

Steve Erwood, The Greenpeace Chronicles. *Greenpeace*, 2011 (pdf). At https://www.greenpeace.org/archive-international/Global/international/publications/other/Greenpeace-Chronicles.pdf. Accessed June 5, 2018.

Greg Haymes, "Audience Participation Key to Music For People." *The Times Union* (Albany, NY), March 24, 1994, P8.

Duncan Heining, "Paul Winter Sextet: Count Me In." *All About Jazz*, October 13, 2016, https://www.allaboutjazz.com/paul-winter-sextet-count-me-in-paul-winter-by-duncan-heining.php?page=1. Accessed June 5, 2018.

Emil A. Holz, "The Schools Band Contest of America (1923)", *Journal of Research in Music Education* 10:1, Spring, 2009, 3. https://www.lipscomb.edu/wind-bandhistory/rhodeswindband_09_americanschoolband.htm. Accessed June 5, 2018.

Harold Howland, "Master Percussionist: Oregon's Collin Walcott." *Modern Drummer*. June 1981. https://www.moderndrummer.com/article/june-1981-master-percussionist-oregons-collin-walcott. Accessed May 16, 2018.

John V. Hurst, "Paul Winter Plays 'Quiet 'Music to Wake People Up." *The Sacramento Bee*, December 21, 1986, EN1.

*The Indianapolis Star*, Sunday, June 4, 1961, Section 8, Entertainment, 131, https://www.newspapers.com/newspage/106825200. Accessed June 5, 2018.

International Society of Bassists, 2017 Convention Presenter Glen Moore, biography. https://www.isbworldoffice.com/convention-presenters.asp?action=view&ProposalID=380. Accessed July 23, 2017.

Bob Keefer, "Paul Winter's version of the Mass celebrates the sounds of nature." *The Register-Guard* (Eugene, OR). March 9, 2006, 1E.

John F. Kennedy Presidential Library and Museum website," Jacqueline Kennedy Entertains," https://www.jfklibrary.org/Asset-Viewer/DXv-zWQOkUmuHblQTJKElw.aspx (video). Accessed June 5, 2018.

Mary W. Kime, "Missa Gaia: Earth Mass by Paul Winter and The Paul Winter Consort." *Environmental Review (*ER) 7:1. *Papers from the First International Conference on Environmental History.* New York: Oxford University Press, Spring, 1983, 124-126.

Tom Knapp, feature article on Paul Winter, *Rambles*, Winter 1999, http://www.rambles.net/paul_winter_1999.html. Accessed June 5, 2018.

Erich Klinghammer and Leslie Laidlaw, "Analysis of 23 Months of Daily Howl Records in a Captive Grey Wolf Pack (Canis Lupus)." The Behavior and Ecology of Wolves *Proceedings of the Symposium on the Behavior and Ecology of Wolves*, 1975. New York: Garland STPM Press, 1979, 153-181.

Bernie Krause, *The Great Animal Orchestra: Finding the Origins of Music in the World's Wild Places*, New York: Back Bay Books, 2012.

Bernie Krause, *Voices of the Wild: Animal Songs, Human Din, and the Call to Save Natural Soundscapes.* New Haven: Yale University Press, 2015.

Betty Dietz Krebs, "Paul Winter Consort Naturally in Tune No Matter the Season." *Dayton Daily News*, September 20, 1991, 25.

Larry The O, "To Sir With Love." *Emusician*, January 7, 2009.

http://www.emusician.com/gear/1332/to-sir-with-love/40689.
Accessed June 5, 2018.

John C. Lilly, "Toward a Cetacean Nation," in Toni Frohoff and
Brenda Peterson, ed., Between Species: Celebrating the Dolphin-
Human Bond. San Francisco: Sierra Club Books, 2003, 77-85.

Dario Martinelli, *how musical is a whale?: Towards a Theory of
Zoomusicology*. Helsinki: International Semiotics Institute, 2002.

Joan McIntyre, "Mind Play," Joan McIntyre, assembler, *Mind in the
Waters: A Book to Celebrate the Consciousness of Whales and Dolphins*.
New York: Charles Scribner's Sons/San Francisco: Sierra Club
Books, 1974, 94.

Jeff McLaughlin, "Paul Winter's Voyages," *Boston Globe*. April 28,
1988, 90.

Bill McQuay and Christopher Joyce, "It Took A Musician's Ear To
Decode The Complex Song In Whale Calls" NPR radio interview,
August 6, 2015. http://www.npr.org/2015/08/06/427851306/it-took-a-
musicians-ear-to-decode-the-complex-song-in-whale-calls. Accessed October 28, 2017.

David L. Mech, "Alpha status, dominance, and division of labor in
wolf packs." *Canadian Journal of Zoology* 77, 1999, 1196-1203.

David L. Mech, "Leadership in Wolf, Canis lupus, Packs." *Canadian
Field-Naturalist* 114(2), 2000, 259-263.

Meagan Meehan, "Interview with musician Paul Winter, leader of
the Paul Winter Consort." *AXS*, November 26, 2016.
https://www.axs.com/interview-with-musician-paul-winter-leader-
of-the-paul-winter-consort-110597#slide=1. Accessed June 5, 2018.

*The Modesto Bee*, "Brown hosts a whale of a celebration, says impact could spread over globe," November 21, 1976.

Jim Mockford, "Rolling Coconut Review Japan Concert April 10 1977." mockford (blog), October 20, 2012. https://mockford.word-press.com/2012/10/20/rolling-coconut-review-japan-concert-april-10-1977/. Accessed October 28, 2017.

Glen Moore website: Origin Arts, Artist Biography 2017. https://thinkns.com/artists/glen-moore/, http://originarts.com/art-ists/artist.php?Artist_ID=296. Accessed June 5, 2018.

Music for People website, http://www.musicforpeople.org/wp/. Accessed November 20, 2017.

National Oceanic and Atmospheric Administration, Alaska Fisheries Science Center, Marine Mammal Laboratory's Marine Mammal Education Web. https://www.afsc.noaa.gov/nmml/education/ceta-ceans/baleen1.php. Accessed October 30, 2017.

The New York Times (obituary). "Collin Walcott, a Co-Founder of 'World Music 'Ensemble. 'November 10, 1984. https://www.ny-times.com/1984/11/10/obituaries/collin-walcott-a-co-founder-of-world-music-ensemble.html. Accessed May 16, 2018.

Jim Nollman, *The Charged Border: Where Whales and Humans Meet*, New York: Henry Holt and Company, 1999).

Oregon website, band biographies, http://oregonband.com/bio/paul-mccandless/. Accessed June 5, 2018.

Joan Duncan Oliver, "Earth Sounds: Paul Winter's Music Celebrates All of Earth's Creatures." *Wildlife Conservation*, July/August 1992, 76-77, 90-91.

*Orlando Sentinel*, May 31, 1985, "John Harris, 50, Known As 'Wolf-man'" (obituary). http://articles.orlandosentinel.com/1985-05-31/news/0300280025_1_carnegie-hall-harris-species-act. Accessed June 5, 2018.

James Oshinsky, *Return to Child: Music for People's Guide to Improvising Music and Authentic Group Leadership*, Goshen, CT: Music for People, 2017 (10th Anniversary Edition).

Patty Lee Parmalee," Interview: A Conversation with Paul Winter." *The Saxophone Symposium*, Summer 1990, 7-19.

Payne, K., Tyack, P., Payne, R., "Progressive Changes in the Songs of Humpback Whales (*Megaptera novaeangliae*): A Detailed Analysis of Two Seasons in Hawaii," Payne, R., ed., *Communication and Behavior of Whales*, Boulder: Westview Press, 1983.

Roger Payne and Scott McVay, "Songs of humpback whales," *Science* 173: 585-597, 1971.

Leonid Pereverzev, "Our Common Ground: Paul Winter in the USSR." *Soviet Life*, June 1987.

Anil Prasad, Ralph Towner: Sense and sensitivity." 2010. http://www.innerviews.org/inner/towner2.html. Accessed June 5, 2018.

Bob Protzman, "Cellist Friesen Takes Music Into A New Age," *The Chicago Tribune* (Knight-Ridder Newspapers syndicated column), December 11, 1986, 60.

Railroad City website, http://www.railroadcity.com/visit/museum/; http://www.ilovealtoona.com/history/. http://www.railroadcity.com/visit/world-famous-horseshoe-curve/. Accessed June 5, 2018.

David S. Rotenstein, "Paul Winter's Jam Sessions with Wolves." December 4, 1994, Pittsburgh Post-Gazette, L-1.

David Rothenberg, *Thousand Mile Song: Whale Music in a Sea of Sound.* New York: Basic Books, 2008.

David Rothenberg, *Whale Music: Thousand Mile Songs in a Sea of Sound,* Newark: Terra Nova Press, 2023.

Theresa Schiavone, "Grand Canyon Suite," All Things Considered, NPR Radio, 2000. Transcript at https://www.npr.org/2000/10/29/1113160/grand-canyon-suite. Accessed November 29, 2017.

Schumacher Center for a New Economics website (about Lindisfarne): *http://www.centerforneweconomics.org/content/lindisfarne-tapes.* Accessed January 21, 2025.

Paul Shepard, *The Others: How Animals Made Us Human.* Washington, D.C.: Island Press, 1996.

Sam Silver and Adi Gevins, *Berkeley Barb,* "Breaking The Species Barrier: California Celebrates The Whales," November 25, 1976.

John Sutphen, "Body State Communication Among Cetaceans," Joan McIntyre, "assembler," *Mind in the Waters: A Book to Celebrate the Consciousness of Whales and Dolphins.* New York: Charles Scribner's Sons/San Francisco: Sierra Club Books, 1974, 141-142.

Richard Sutherland, "Animals in the Mix: Interspecies music and recording." *Social Alternatives* 33:1, 2014, 25; 23-29.

*Symphony News,* "New Programming Ideas: Creative Captivation: Paul Winter," February, 1980.

Jeffrey Taylor, "Paul Winter." *Contemporary musicians: profiles of the people in music.* 10, 1994, 266-268.

Ralph Towner website, http://www.ralphtowner.com. Accessed June 5, 2018.

Stephen Trimble, "Paul Winter's Canyon Consort," *Sierra Club Bulletin*, March/April 1986, 59-62.

Nicholas Tuff, "An interview with Paul Winter." Paul Winter Updates, Solstice (web), Dec 10, 2014. http://www.paulwinter.com/winterviews-2014/. Accessed June 5, 2018.

Dale Turner, "Ralph Towner's Nylon and 12-String Craftsmanship." July 14, 2016, *Guitar World.* http://www.guitarworld.com/lessons-acoustic-lessons/ralph-towners-nylon-and-12-string-craftsmanship/29450. Accessed June 5, 2018.

Umission, "Person of the Week: Paul Winter: Musician, Soprano Saxophonist, Pioneer of world music celebrating the earth and community of life." Web – date? http://umission.org/person-of-the-week/paul-winter/. Accessed June 5, 2018.

Joseph Vella, "Interview: Paul Winter–The 16th Annual Summer Solstice Concert June 18th NYC." *Huffpost New York,* 2012.

Tony Vellela, "Paul Winter Consort Rings in the Solstice – Before diversity became a buzzword, the composer's 'world music 'tapped into many cultures and rituals." *Christian Science Monitor,* December 16, 1993, 16.

Elizabeth F. von Bergen, "Interview with Paul Winter." *The Instrument*, May 1977.

Peter Warshall, "The Ways of Whales," Joan McIntyre, ed., *Mind in the Waters: A Book to Celebrate the Consciousness of Whales and Dolphins*. New York: Charles Scribner's Sons/San Francisco: Sierra Club Books, 1974, 110-140.

Paul Weideman, "Paul McCandless – Horns of Plenty." *The Santa Fe New Mexican*, July 23, 2004, Pasatiempo, 32.

Rex Weyler, "Waves of Compassion: The founding of Greenpeace. Where Are They Now?" Utne Reader, 2003, http://www.utne.com/community/wavesofcompassion. Accessed October 28, 2017.

Paul Winter, *Common Ground* (CD), 1978, liner notes.

Paul Winter, *Callings* (CD), 1980, liner notes.

Paul Winter, *Missa Gaia/Earth Mass* (CD), 1982, liner notes.

Paul Winter website: milestones, http://www.paulwinter.com/paul-winter/milestones. Accessed June 5, 2018.

Paul Winter, program notes, "Paul Winter Consort at Princeton University Chapel." Friday, Oct. 8, 1982.

Paul Winter SoundPlay website. http://www.paulwinter.com/adventures-in-soundplay/. Accessed June 5, 2018.

Paul Winter SoundPlay workshop, memo page. http://www.paulwinter.com/adventures-in-soundplay/post-workshop-memo-by-paul-winter. Accessed June 5, 2018.

*Whole Earth Review*," Number 61, "Paul Winter," 1988, 135.

About the Author

**Bob Gluck** is a pianist, composer, and author of three books published by the University of Chicago Press, *You'll Know When You Get There: Herbie Hancock and the Mwandishi Band* (2012), T*he Miles Davis 'Lost 'Quintet and Other Revolutionary Ensembles* (2016), and *Pat Metheny, Stories beyond Words* (2024).

Among his recent recordings is *Infinite Spirit: Revisiting Music of the Mwandishi Band* (FMR 2016, with Billy Hart, Eddie Henderson, and Christopher Dean Sullivan) and *Early Morning Star* (FMR 2020).

Bob Gluck is Professor Emeritus of Music at the University at Albany in Albany, New York.